THE HARDING SISTERS

REVISITED

THE HARDING SISTERS

REVISITED

CAROL E. PLIMPTON

Primix Publishing
11620 Wilshire Blvd
Suite 900, West Wilshire Center, Los Angeles, CA, 90025
www.primixpublishing.com
Phone: 1-800-538-5788

Published by Primix Publishing   11/03/2021

ISBN: 978-1-955177-55-9(sc)
ISBN: 978-1-955177-56-6(e)

Library of Congress Control Number: 2021924113

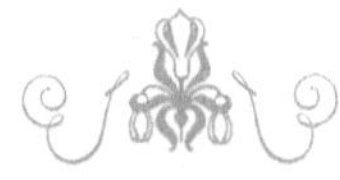

CONTENTS

PROLOGUE

If one approaches Sterling City Road from the South part of Lyme, it runs approximately three miles from its junction with Connecticut Route 156, at the Tiffany Farms, to its end, again rejoining Route 156 at the center of Hamburg, by the Grange Hall. There are two boatyards on the cove, and the water flows between the cove and the Connecticut River. There is a general store, H.L. Reynolds & Co., a public hall and a Congregational Church on Route 156 in Hamburg. A volunteer fire department is an integral part of the town. Sterling City Road has many homes, but the majority of original structures remain. It is within the boundaries of this road that this story begins.

The Harding family lived in a large white farmhouse next to the Mill Pond where Sterling City takes a leisurely turn from the Northeast to the Northwest. Lyman and Nora Harding were the parents to eleven children, Florence, Helen, Kate, Maria, Elsie, Mae, Tess, Ruth, Lyman, Hazel, and Grace. The births of the children began in March 1883 with the arrival of Florence and spanned 19 years through January 1902 when Grace was born. In March of 1896, Nora gave birth to the first son who lived only three days. He had been named Lyman Noah Harding, so when the second boy was born in June 1900, he was also named Lyman, but had the middle name of Darius. As patriarch of the family, Lyman the elder was delighted to hear of the birth of another son. And so the Harding family becomes the background of this story.

The girls grew up and left home, several making their homes on Sterling City Road. Helen and husband, Hal Martin, Ruth, Hazel and husband Clarence Lee, and Grace and husband, Al Hendry, all became permanent residents of Sterling City Road. Florence and husband, Fred Fitts, lived in Eagleville, CT; Kate and husband, D.G. Reynolds, lived directly at the intersection of

Sterling City Road and Route 156; Tess and husband, Bill Peck, lived at Early Dawn Farm about two mile south of Sterling City Road on Route 156; Elsie and husband, Harry Clark, lived in Niantic, a town to the East; and Mae and husband Frank Jones, as well as Maria and husband Egbert Bull, lived in Ivoryton, "across the river." Lyman, the only son, died at age 24.

CHAPTER ONE

Grace

When Grace, the youngest of the Harding girls, finished her schooling at the one-room schoolhouse on Sterling City Road in June of 1920, she was dating Reg Stark, one of Lyme's native sons. She told her parents that she wanted to go to nursing school in Hartford.

"I know that my sisters have chosen other directions, but I want to be a nurse." She announced at the dinner table. "I want to go to Hartford Hospital School of Nursing."

Lyman smiled as he looked at his youngest daughter. "So you have ambitions that we haven't heard about before, Grace. Where did you come by such an idea?"

"I want to help others and I think I can do a good job with the ailing and sick people. It would be a good career for me."

"You would have to live in Hartford," her mother, Nora, stated. "How much will this cost?"

"Well, I already have a roommate lined up, so the living cost would be minimal. And the tuition is just $200 a year. The program would be two years."

"You would live at the school?"

"Yes there is a dormitory associated with it. My meals would be included in the housing. That would be another $200 a year. And I could get a job so you wouldn't have any other expenses from the $400. I might be able to earn the second year's $400 while I am working and going to school. I could pay you back when I start working as a nurse."

"What does Reg think about this, Grace?"

"Oh, Mother, what does it matter? We can see each other on holidays. It's not as if we were engaged to be married. Reg wants to go on to school too."

Lyman leaned back in his chair, folding his arms in front of him. "What do you think, Lyman, about your baby sister becoming a nurse?"

Young Lyman replied, "I think it is a great idea, Father. I could work harder on the farm so we can afford to send her to school! I think we should help her do it."

Grace beamed. Her plan was going to come true. She would be able to live away from home, and when she finished nursing school she could marry Reg and then she would never have to live at home again. It wasn't that living at home was that horrible but she wanted to make her own decisions in life and not have a parent looking over her shoulder. Being the youngest, she had put up with the hand-me-downs and the expectations of her older siblings. The only sister she could seem to manipulate with any regularity was Hazel. And Hazel was married and living on her own.

*****

The day before Grace was to depart for Hartford, she was in her bedroom packing. Reg was leaning against the door jam watching.

"Nothing I have is good enough for Hartford," she bemoaned. "All I have are these hand-me-downs."

Reg picked up a dress from the bed. "I always liked this one."

"That was Hazel's. Do you know that nothing I own is mine? The first thing I am going to do when I become a nurse is to buy a pretty dress."

Reg smiled. "I can't wait to see it on you!"

"Or off me?" She gave a devilish smile.

Grace beckoned to Reg to join her on the bed.

Reg feigned shock. "But your parents are home!"

"Everyone is outside. No one will know."

They kiss passionately and start disrobing as they move toward the bed…

*****

On the day of departure the family gathered outside the farmhouse to say good-bye. Lyman had hitched up the team of horses to the large wagon and waited to load Grace, her suitcase, young Lyman, Nora and Ruth to head to Hartford to see Grace start her career. Grace noted that Clarence's truck was parked next to the wagon. She went to Hazel and gave her a hug, whispering in her ear, "Thanks so much."

Hazel looked confused. "For what?"

"The truck is not for me? Clarence isn't taking me?"

"Father is taking you in the wagon."

"But the truck would be faster!"

Lyman approached. "Clarence's truck is for business only. This wagon has never let me down. Let's get going. We have forty miles to cover."

Lyman took her suitcase and tossed it in the wagon. Nora, Ruth and young Lyman were already in the wagon.

*****

Dusty and exhausted, the Hardings arrived in front of the dormitory where Grace was to live. They made their way to the austere dorm room she would share with another girl.

Lyman looked it over. "Are you sure you want this, Grace?"

"I am."

"All right." He hugged his daughter. "Make us proud!"

Each of them hugged Grace and left the room. She closed the door and leaned on it with a sigh of relief. "I am finally free."

*****

Grace did well in nursing school. She came home for holidays, getting rides from families of fellow students, and avoiding the horse and wagon commute. She was happy with her choice and she had met several fellows throughout her first year. Reg was an apprentice to an electrician in the Lyme area, and he was getting his education first hand. Even though Grace met others, she still fancied Reg and was sure to see him each holiday.

The second year in nursing school was more difficult. Grace found she had to study as well as perform the practical duties of a real nurse. She found herself being tense as well as feeling ill in the mornings, and she was tired all the time. When she missed her period, she knew what the problem was. She decided to confide in her sister, Mae.

Grace traveled home for the week-end, and she asked

her brother-in-law, Clarence, to take her to see Mae in Ivoryton in his truck. He did as she asked despite Hazel wanting to know what was going on. "I will go too, to see Mae and Frank," Hazel said, suspicious of Grace's intentions with her husband.

"No, Hazel," Clarence said. There is just not enough room with all the tools and wood. I don't have time to clear them all out. I will just take her over there and I will visit with Frank. We will be back early."

Hazel scoffed, "I just don't know what could be so secret that she had to go to talk to Mae." Hazel did not like being kept in the dark. Hazel immediately went to the telephone to ask the other sisters what they thought.

When Clarence and Grace arrived at Mae and Frank's, Frank was out in his woodworking shop so Clarence joined him there. Grace went into the house and out to the glassed-in side porch where Mae sat, sewing a sampler.

She gave Mae a hug. "How are you doing, Mae?" she asked.

"Pretty good," Mae replied. She was short and a bit round, and she had a blue spot on one cheek. Her hair was in a braid wrapped around her head. "How is school going for you?"

"Oh, Mae. Something terrible has happened," Grace started to cry. "I missed my period this month, and I had to tell someone. I knew you wouldn't share this, especially with Mother and Father."

Mae reached over and handed Grace a handkerchief. "Honey, did you see a doctor?"

"No. I needed to talk to you first."

"Is the baby Reg's?"

"No, oh I don't know, maybe…"

"Grace! What have you been doing? How could you not know whose baby it is?"

"Well I met a couple of nice fellows…"

"Grace! You should not share yourself like that! You should save yourself for your husband!" Mae exclaimed.

"Mae, what am I going to do? I can't raise a baby on my own. I am still in school. I need to get out and work; to live my life. Who is going to marry someone with a baby? A child?"

"Okay, Grace, this is what will happen. You will call me when you have the baby. Frank and I will come to Hartford and we will adopt the child. We can't have children so this will be a blessing for us. No one need know the circumstances, but you will have to avoid coming home as the pregnancy starts to show. Just tell Mother and Father that you have so much work to do that you cannot take time off. You will have to be very careful not to tell anyone else. In the meantime I will express the thought that we may adopt. Does this help?"

"Oh yes, Mae! I knew you would think of something! That could just work…" Grace dried her eyes. She was glad she was not living at home when all of this happened as she would have a very hard time hiding it. She knew her sisters would be critical of her. Her parents would be so disappointed in her. Thank goodness Mae was there to help her out.

She hugged Mae good-bye and went out to fetch Clarence from the shop. She nodded to Frank. "Let's go, Clarence. I am sure Hazel is anxious to have you home."

Off they went, and Grace did not say a word the entire way home. Clarence didn't mind as he was a quiet fellow.

*****

Grace spent the rest of the week-end visiting sisters and her parents. Her ride picked her up on Sunday afternoon. "See you soon, dear," Nora called as she waved.

Thanksgiving came and Grace felt she was still able to go home without showing her pregnancy. The family all gathered at the homestead for dinner. They had a fine time and were settled down in the living area, chatting and joking with each other. "Oh this is so nice," Nora exclaimed, "I can hardly wait for Christmas."

Mae and Grace exchanged knowing looks. Grace would be six months pregnant at that time. She doubted she would be able to pull it off. But no one mentioned her gaining weight or any other signs of her pregnancy. Hazel kept a wary eye on Grace and noticed the non-verbal exchange between Mae and Grace.

Later, at home, Hazel asked Clarence again why Grace had gone to visit Mae. "How do I know, Hazel?" He seemed frustrated. "I was in the shop with Frank. I don't know what they talked about. Why is this bothering you so much?"

"Because there is something going on between the two of them, " she retorted. "They have some kind of secret. I noticed how they looked at each other when Mother mentioned Christmas."

"Maybe they are making some sort of surprise for the family, or for your mother, for the holiday," he suggested.

"I don't think so," Hazel replied.

December came and so did Christmas. Grace had put on some weight but she dressed in looser clothes and came home for the holiday. Nora remarked when she saw her, "Looks as if the food must be pretty good at nursing school, Grace. You have put on some weight, I see."

"Um, yes I have. I think the stress of the schooling this term is causing me to eat more, Mother. I will be careful." She folded her arms and smiled.

The family came again for the holiday and the meal was pleasant. Hazel sat next to Grace and said "So, you've been stressed at school, Mother said."

"Yes, Hazel, not only the book work is difficult but I am dealing with patients each and every day as well as doing my night waitressing job. I guess I am a stress eater."

"Well you ate like a bird today," Hazel huffed. Grace sensed Hazel may have suspicions.

"Have you seen Reg since you have been home?" Hazel asked.

"I will see him tomorrow before I head back," Grace answered. "He has been very busy too."

"Then there is no one up in Hartford that you are dating?" Hazel tilted her head and asked.

"No – I am too busy to be seeing anyone up there." Grace squirmed in her chair.

"Oh," Hazel said, "I thought maybe you and Mae were talking about gentlemen callers that you had met."

"Really? When?"

"When you had Clarence take you over to see Mae last August."

"For heaven's sake, Hazel, I can hardly remember having Clarence take me to Mae's, much less what we talked about. Must you be involved in everything that goes on? You are just a busybody." The other sisters laughed gently and Hazel's face reddened.

"Did it ever occur to you that I may be asking because I care about your welfare?"

"I certainly doubt that."

Grace stayed in Hartford for the next three months, replying to the letters that Nora sent, asking her to come home for a visit, by saying her work would soon be done and she would be graduated in May. It was evident to the girls in the nursing school, and to the instructors, that Grace was gaining a lot of weight but she dressed in a way to hide the pregnancy. Her roommate asked her once if she was pregnant. "Good grief, no!" she exclaimed. "I just like to eat!"

In early March Grace awoke in the morning with excruciating pain in her abdominal area. Her roommate had gone home for the week-end so she was alone. She writhed in her bed, rolling and stuffing her pillow in her mouth so she didn't scream and give her secret away. The pains grew worse and after several hours of contractions she could feel her water break. "This is it," she said to herself. She was about to become a mother. She knew there was not time to get to the hospital, nor to ask for help. This had to remain a secret and she would have to find a way to get the baby to Mae. But how? She didn't drive, nor did she have a car. She had nothing for the baby to wear. The contractions came again and Grace tried not to scream. She could feel that the baby was moving down. She gritted her teeth and pushed as hard as she could. All of a sudden there was a huge gush and she felt the baby sliding out of her. The pain became a dull ache. And the baby lay between her legs, a bloody, yellowish color, and appeared to be trying to gasp for breath. It was a girl. "What if she cries?" Grace thought. "People will hear and will find out." There was only one thing to do. She took her pillow and held it over the baby, pushing down hard on the head. She held the pillow there for what seemed hours to her, but was really only about 10 minutes. There was no movement under the pillow. Grace lifted it cautiously and looked at the little girl who lay still on the bed.

"Oh my God!" Grace said to the lifeless form. "What a mess you have made of my life!" She lifted the baby in a sheet and carried her to the desk where she had some scissors to cut the umbilical cord. She knew she had to clamp it off and did so by tying it with string. Then, leaving the baby on the desk in the sheet she made her way to the bathroom: she knew from her training that the afterbirth needed to pass. Luckily no one was in the hallway as she made her way to the bathroom. There she sat and forced the afterbirth. Someone had left a towel in the bathroom so Grace got into the shower and cleaned herself up. She made her way quietly back to her room.

Grace felt weak and nauseous as she wrapped the baby more closely in the sheets. She then went to the window and looked to see if there were many people outside. The garbage bin was just outside the back door of the dormitory. She would have to go down two flights of stairs, and then the door would be to her right. She was lucky it was early on a Saturday morning and most girls slept in. Many weren't even there as they had gone home for the week-end. She dressed quickly and wrapped the sheet and baby in a brown bed cover and made her way out the door, down the stairs, through the outside door and to the dumpster. She reached up and dropped the package into it. They she headed back to her room, sure that no one suspected anything. She pulled the remainder of sheets off her bed and scrubbed the mattress where some stains had appeared. Her roommate would not be back until Sunday so she had time to get things in order. Then she lay down on her roommate's bed and went to sleep.

She slept most of the day; she was not hungry and had no desire to get up. But she needed to get the room back in order and so she could rest easy that her roommate would not suspect anything. She brought out her second set of sheets and made her bed. She checked the carpet and the desk for any signs of blood. She was assured that she had everything under control. "Oh no – now what will I tell Mae?"

Later on Sunday she decided she would call Mae and tell her the baby had been stillborn. She went to use the hall telephone and looked to see if others were around. No one was there so she dialed Mae's number. The phone rang about five times and then Mae answered. "Hello?"

"It's Grace, Mae."

"Hi Grace – It is good to hear from you. How is everything going?"

Grace thought she should try to cry but that emotion

was not there for her. "Um Mae, I have something awful to tell you."

"What has happened?"

"The baby was stillborn. She came yesterday."

"Oh Grace! Are you in the hospital?"

"No, I did not have time to get there. Everything happened very quickly."

A little girl, Mae thought. "How sad!"

"Yes," Grace said. "I am so sorry for you."

"For me? What about what you went through?"

"I am okay, just tired out. Perhaps it was for the best."

"… odd thing to say," Mae thought, but she kept talking to Grace and encouraging her to come home soon.

"Oh I will come next week-end," Grace said. "I miss everyone so much. I will see you then."

"All right, Grace. Try to be strong."

When the conversation was over, Grace smiled and walked back to her room.

When Mae hung up the telephone there were tears in her eyes. Frank came in and said "Who was on the telephone?"

"Grace." She said quietly.

"What's wrong?"

"Our baby was stillborn. It was a little girl, Frank. We would have had a little girl to love and raise."

Frank shook his head. "What did the doctor tell her?"

"There was no doctor. I guess she gave birth in her dormitory. She was all alone."

"What did she do?"

"I guess she didn't tell me – I didn't ask because I was so shocked. My poor baby sister had to go through that all by herself."

Frank shook his head. "Well it's Sunday and we usually head over the river to visit the Lyme sisters. Do you feel like going?" he asked.

"Yes, or they will think something is wrong. It will be hard to be with Mother and Father though. I know they will ask about Grace because they miss her so much."

Frank went out to get the Plymouth out of the garage and Mae went to get her hat. She took her purse from the end table and went outside to the car. She hoped she could hide her sorrow from the others.

CHAPTER TWO

Mae

In the summer of 1918, Mae and Frank met each other at the Hamburg Fair. Mae was working the chicken barbecue dinner and Frank was sitting with friends, enjoying the meal. Mae was serving his table and he thought, "Now this is a really nice girl! So pretty!" He decided it would be a good thing to make her acquaintance. So, when dessert was served he said, "Can you take a break and join me for dessert?" Mae looked startled, as she had also noticed the dashing Frank and wondered who he was. She had never seen him in Lyme before.

He smiled at her and winked. Mae blushed. "Well, I guess I could take a break. That pie surely is tasty."

Frank pulled out the empty chair next to him as Mae made her way to the pie table, and returned with a slice of apple crumb pie. "I told them I was taking a break," she giggled.

Frank looked at her with a broad smile, "I am Frank Jones, and you are…?"

"Mae Harding."

"Pleased to meet you, Mae. I didn't expect to meet someone so pretty and charming today!"

Mae blushed. "Thank you. It is nice to meet you. Do you live in Lyme?"

"I live in Ivoryton."

"Oh, my sister's fiancé lives in Ivoryton. Perhaps you know him? Egbert Bull?"

"I do indeed. I have a store in the center of Ivoryton – kind of a general store, and Egbert comes in frequently. The Bull family is well known. What is your sister's name?"

"Maria."

"Are there just the two of you in the family?"

Mae laughed, "Heavens no! I have nine sisters and a brother!"

"Oh my!" Frank said with raised eyebrows. "That is a large family!"

"Yes, we live here on Sterling City Road in a big old farmhouse."

"So your father is a farmer?"

"Yes. We all help out in one way or another."

"Is your family here at the fair?"

"Every last one of them! The fair is the best day of the year here in Lyme. We all volunteer to do something, and we love to watch the oxen pulls and horse pulls. And there is square dancing at night after the dinner!"

"Really? Would you go square dancing with me- or – I didn't really ask if you were seeing anyone…"

Mae blushed again. "No I am not seeing anyone right now. Three of my sisters, Florence, Helen, and Kate are married. Hazel is dating Clarence Lee, Elsie is dating Harry Clark, Maria is dating Egbert, Tess is dating Bill Peck, and Ruth and Grace are also not dating right now. My brother is seeing Dorothy Latham. So that is a long answer to your question."

"Well, I would like to take you square dancing if you would do me the honor of joining me."

"I would love to," Mae smiled. "My volunteer shift ends in half an hour. Would you like to go watch the oxen pull with me then? And when the square dancing starts we can come back here. Dick Lee is the caller and he is terrific!"

"That sounds wonderful. And I am just going to sit right here and sip coffee until you are ready to go." Frank wanted to keep his eye on this pretty, funny girl. He had a feeling that she was the one for him.

Mae waved and went back to the serving table to finish her duties.

The oxen pull was fun and Frank was introduced to some of the family: Hazel and her beau, Clarence, Tess and hers, Bill, Ruth, Grace, and the patriarchs, Nora and Lyman. Young Lyman was also there. Frank was very polite and he was intrigued by all of the family dynamics.

"So, Frank," Hazel said, "Have you lived in Ivoryton all your life?"

"I have. My family ran the store that I currently have. They keep an eye on me though!" He laughed.

"Do you make a lot of money?" Hazel asked.

"Hazel! That is a rude question, Grace exclaimed. "Sorry, Frank, Hazel is always into someone else's business."

"I am not," said Hazel. "I am thinking about Mae and how he will take care of her."

Mae jumped in and said shyly, "Well we just met. You may be rushing things."

She looked at Frank and again he winked at her. "I think I hear the square dance music starting. Shall we go?"

"We are coming too," Hazel said. "Dick Lee is Clarence's cousin. He is a wonderful caller."

"So Mae told me," Frank replied.

"We are right behind you," Tess said. "Mother, are you and Father coming?"

"We will be there soon. Frank, it was very nice to meet you!" Nora said.

"And you as well, Mrs. Harding." Frank knew what to say when; he believed he had found the girl of his dreams, love at first sight, and he knew he must impress the parents in order to ask for Mae's hand in marriage, if it went that far. But Frank knew then and there that Mae was the girl for him. It was a case of love at first sight.

Within a week she became Maisie and he was Jonesie. They saw each other whenever they could. Mae was teaching school and Frank had to run his store but the evenings and week-ends were theirs. Her sisters teased her about rushing into romance and they worried a bit about her because she was very naïve. But they were happy for her and everyone liked Jonesie!

*****

In September, Frank decided it was time to approach Maisie's parents and ask for her hand in marriage. He wanted their approval before proposing to Maisie. He left the store in the hands of his assistant and drove over to Lyme at noon. He knew that Lyman would be in from the fields for lunch and he wanted to go when Mae was at school.

He pulled in to the Harding Homestead on Sterling City Road. As he got out of the car he saw Lyman crossing from the barn to the farmhouse. "Good timing," he thought. As he approached the back door he took in a deep breath. "Here goes," he said to himself.

Nora and Lyman were alone at the kitchen table. "Frank!" Nora exclaimed. "How nice to see you! Will you have some lunch with us?"

"No thanks, Mrs. Harding," Frank said, "I've come to speak with you both about Maisie."

"Is something wrong?" Nora asked, with fear in her eyes.

"Oh no – nothing like that."

"That's good, " Lyman said quietly, continuing to eat his lunch.

"Mr. and Mrs. Harding, I've come here to tell you that I love your daughter very much. I would like your permission to ask her to marry me." Frank stood at attention facing the patriarchal couple.

"Which daughter?" Lyman asked.

"Oh Lyman!" Nora said, "He's just teasing, Frank."

Frank wiped his brow.

"Well, Nora, what do you think," Lyman said, "should we let this man take our little Mae to be his bride?"

"I say YES," Nora said with a smile to Frank.

"Then it shall be so," Lyman said, and then went back to eating.

Frank grinned from ear to ear. "I will propose to her tonight then. Thank you so much."

Nora asked, "Since you have known each other a very little time, perhaps the actual wedding should wait for a while. What are your thoughts, Frank?"

"I was thinking that Christmas time would be good."

"What a Christmas we will have! Maria and Egbert are getting married then too! Oh Lyman, what a time we will have!"

Frank again smiled and said that he probably should get back to work. He did not leave the store very often. He was relieved that this formality was done. He said his thank you's and his good-byes. Then he drove off to Ivoryton, practicing what he would say to Maisie.

*****

That evening he put on his best tie and suit and drove back to Lyme. Mae was waiting for him on the porch. He beckoned for her to stay where she was and he made his way to the porch. She was sitting in a rocking chair. He got down on one knee and took her hand. "Maisie, I love you. I have loved you ever since I set eyes on you at the fair. I am hoping that you will agree to be my wife. Will you marry me?" and with his other hand he took a small ring box out of his pocket. Mae opened the box and gasped.

"The ring is beautiful, Jonesie! I love you so much. Yes! I will marry you!" Mae was so excited.

"I asked your parents for your hand in marriage and they said yes," Frank said. "I was so nervous but they were really good to me. Of course your father asked which girl I wanted to marry," Frank chuckled. "But he knew and he was really good about it."

"When do you think we should get married?" Mae asked.

"I think Christmas time," Frank said. "It would be such a special Christmas!"

"Maria and Egbert are getting married December 24. I wonder…."

"Wonder what?"

"I wonder if they would want to do a double wedding! It would be very special. Would that be okay with you, Frank?"

"Anything you want is okay with me, Maisie."

"Oh, Frank, you are so good to me." She was admiring the ring on her finger. "Let's go see Maria and Egbert now – they are actually in the parlor with Mother."

"Wow," Frank thought, "This is like a whirlwind now!"

When Mae and Frank entered the parlor, the three looked up expectantly. "Well?" Nora said.

"Frank asked me to marry him and I said yes!" Mae exclaimed. "Look at the ring, Mother, isn't it beautiful?"

Maria came over to see the ring as well and she hugged her sister. "This is wonderful, Mae. When will you marry?"

"Well, Frank wants to get married at Christmas time. And I know you and Egbert have set the date of the 24th, so maybe…"

Maria interrupted. "We can have a double wedding! Let's do it! Father can walk us down the aisle, one on each arm! How fun would that be?"

"Are the church aisles big enough for three abreast?" Mae laughed.

Mae and Maria spent hours discussing the wedding plans. All of the sisters would be the attendants and they asked the two eldest, Florence and Helen, to be the matrons of honor. Doad and Carol Reynolds would be the flower girls.

The months flew by. December arrived before they realized, but they were ready. The double wedding was the talk of Lyme. The brides had matching gowns, and the bridesmaids wore a light blue, with the matrons of honor in a darker blue. The family and townspeople all assembled in the First Congregational Church of Lyme. Young Lyman was an usher with Frank's brother and Egbert's two brothers.

When the music started, Doad and Carol walked in the left aisle, strewing rose petals, then the sisters, led by the matrons of honor, came down both aisles of the church. Then Lyman entered with his daughters on his arms and walked them down the left aisle to the altar. He left them with their intended husbands and joined Nora in the first pew. It was a beautiful wedding and a reception followed at the Harding Homestead. The house was filled with people and desserts were served. The girls had been baking for days and had made an assortment of treats for the wedding guests. Coffee or tea accompanied the desserts.

After an hour, the newly married couples departed for their honeymoons: Egbert and Maria to Boston, and Frank and Mae to Niagara Falls. They would be gone a week. Everyone agreed it had been a lovely wedding.

CHAPTER THREE

Frank and Mae

On Sundays, Mae and Frank would make their way across the river to Lyme to visit. They always saved Tess and Bill for last on their visiting routine, because by then they would have been served enough tea and would not have to be exposed to Tess' serving all from one teabag, often a used one at that. Ruth was living with Tess and Bill at that time when she was home from business school. She would not be there on this particular Sunday as she had some exams to prepare for, and she decided to stay in New York. Ruth, Grace and Lyman had yet to marry and it looked as if Ruth was choosing career over marriage. Since Grace was still dating Reg, the family assumed she would do her nursing and then be married. Lyman was still dating Dorothy Latham.

So Frank pulled the car into the driveway of the old homestead to start with the Hardings, and then if any others were there, they could skip going to their homes. In fact, Harry's car was in the yard and so they knew Elsie was visiting as well. That would be good because they did not often go to Niantic to see Elsie and Harry as it was too far.

Mae and Frank went up the steps to the front porch and in the front door to the parlor. "Hello Mother, Father," Mae said. "And good to see you too Elsie and Harry!" They were greeted warmly and Mae could see that young Lyman was just coming in from the barn. Mother went to the kitchen to get the tea.

They visited about their week and who had heard from whom. They reviewed the comings and goings of the Rands and the Lathams who lived on the portion of the road that was actually called Sterling City. Mother talked about how she hoped Grace would come home to visit the next week-end; Ruth had been there the previous one. It was hard for Nora to think of her girls as career women when she had been a housewife all of her life. Raising children was her specialty!

"I had hoped we would pick a week-end when Grace would be home," Elsie said. "Ruth as well. They must be busy in school."

At the mention of Grace, Mae and Frank exchanged a quick glance. Mae said "Well I did talk to Grace this week-end. She said she had to study really hard for her exams. I think she did mention coming home next week-end."

"Oh how lovely!" Nora smiled from ear to ear. "I haven't seen her since Christmas and I didn't think she was looking too well at that point. I guess it is hard to do all that studying as well as being on the floor practicing her nursing skills." No one said any more about Grace.

Young Lyman came in after washing up at the kitchen sink. "Hello sisters! Frank, Harry. Welcome to Sunday at the Hardings!"

Elsie asked, "Did you all go to church this morning?"

"Why yes, I went with Lyman," Nora said, " And your father had a good visit with D.G. Kate was at church with little Leland, Doad, Carol and Baby Donna."

"They are all so darling," Mae said, "I don't know how Kate keeps track of so many!"

Nora looked at Mae in astonishment. "Mae, how do you think I managed with ten girls and one boy?" Everyone laughed.

Nora turned to Elsie. "How are Althea and Lucille?"

Elsie smiled. "They are doing well. They are with Harry's mother today, probably being spoiled rotten!

The visit lasted about forty-five minutes and then the Clarks and the Jones' were off to see Hazel and Clarence. Hazel fixed tea for everyone and she had baked some molasses cookies that served as a sweet treat.

They all chatted about the other sisters, their parents, Lyman, Ruth's completion of business school, and Grace's upcoming graduation from nursing school. Again Mae and Frank exchanged a look, and Hazel caught it. "So Mae," she said, "Have you heard from Grace? She has been pretty scarce around here for quite a while."

"Yes, she has had a lot of work to do," Mae replied.

"Too much to come home to spend a day with her Mother and Father? They aren't getting any younger, and they talk about her all the time."

"Well she mentioned coming home next week-end."

"So she doesn't have as much work now?" Hazel pushed. "And that poor boy, Reg. He should be getting fed up with this by now. I don't think he goes to see her."

"No I don't think he does."

"Well, if I were Reg, I would wonder if Grace didn't have another beau on the scene! Hey is that what it is you have been hiding? She has another fellow?" Hazel thought she had hit the nail on the head.

"No she doesn't have another fellow that I know of. And what are you talking about that we have been hiding something?"

Everyone at the table was at attention.

"Oh come on, Mae, you and Grace have had something going for months. When you are together you exchange secretive glances and you whisper when others are around. I know you both too well to think there is nothing going on. I think you know something that we all need to know. There should be no secrets between sisters."

Elsie sat bug-eyed as the tension rose in the room. She did not have a clue as to what was going on. Clarence stared at his teacup, as did Harry and Frank, not wanting to get involved in this. Hazel definitely had a way of stirring up the pot!

"Hazel, there is nothing going on that I know of," Mae said crossly, but there were tears in her eyes.

"If there is nothing, why are you tearful?" Hazel retorted.

"You just have to be in everyone's business, Hazel. If Grace and I have shared something special then it is for us to share and keep."

"So there IS something going on!" Hazel smirked.

Feeling threatened, and unable to contain herself any more, Mae said quietly, "If you must know, Grace had an accident and became pregnant." She then told the story as Frank shook his head. "We were going to adopt the child. But she was stillborn. We cannot let Mother and Father know about this as Grace is shamed enough. And it would just kill Mother to hear this. So see if you can be a good big sister to her and not even bring the subject up when you see Grace. It was to be our secret."

Hazel was momentarily speechless. But she regained her composure quickly. "Was Reg the father? Did he know?"

"I don't know, Hazel. I didn't ask a lot of questions; I was just trying to help our baby sister."

"So Grace didn't come home over the last few months because we would all know…but if she carried a baby nine months, as you say, she would have known it was dead before the birth. And you say she had the baby on her own in the dormitory room? This sounds pretty fishy to me!"

"What are you saying, Hazel?" Mae asked with an edge to her voice.

"You think about it, Mae, and see if you can't figure it out. There was a baby and then there wasn't. She would not make up a story about being pregnant as that was very shameful, even if Reg WAS the father."

"Frank," Mae said quietly, "It is time for us to go. Hazel, you promise me that you are not going to let Grace know that you know anything about this. You promise me right now!"

"All right, Mae, I promise," Hazel said as she crossed her fingers behind her back and smirked.

Mae hustled out with Frank and Elsie looked at Harry as if to say "Let's get out of here." Harry rose.

"Guess we should be moving on, Elsie. Still have

Tess and Bill to see." Hazel just looked at them and Clarence got up to take his teacup to the sink.

"Well, Elsie, nothing to say?" Hazel asked somewhat sarcastically.

"Not much to say, Hazel. It is Grace's business and we should let it be. If she wants any help she will ask. She always has been able to stand up for herself."

"Yes she has," Hazel thought, "Yes she has."

*****

When Elsie and Harry turned into Early Dawn Farm, they noted that Mae and Frank were not there. "Mae was pretty upset," Elsie said, "So I guess they went on home."

"Yep," Harry muttered.

They walked up the steps and into the kitchen to find Tess alone. Bill was apparently working in the fields. They visited over tea made with one teabag and, after reviewing most of the news gained in their visits, carefully avoiding the subject of Grace, they said good-bye and headed back to Niantic. Tess' phone began to ring. It was a single ring so she knew it was hers and not a different party. There were four families on the party line and Tess sometimes sneaked a listen to conversations when she was bored.

"Hello?" she said as she picked up the telephone. It was Hazel.

"Are Mae and Frank still there?" she asked.

"No, they did not come. Just Elsie and Harry and they left a few minutes ago. They said Mae had been at your house but she didn't come here. I guess they had enough Sunday visiting."

Well...." Hazel began, "Mae was pretty upset when she left here. You know how I was saying that Grace and Mae had something going on?"

"Yes, I know you thought that; but you are always into somebody's business and you don't always get the stories straight!"

"This time my intuition paid off." Hazel ignored the comment about her being a busybody.

"Really."

"Yes, really. Did you know that Grace hasn't been home in a long time because she was PREGNANT?"

"What?"

"Yes. And we don't know who the father was. And the baby was stillborn according to Grace and what she told Mae. Mae was going to adopt the baby and they were going to hide all of this."

"I didn't think Grace looked well at Christmas but I never suspected that she and Reg would have, you know, gotten together."

"Mae didn't say it was Reg. She didn't know who it was."

"Well that makes it even worse. If Grace didn't know who the father was then she was, well, getting together with more than one man. This will kill Mother when she hears."

"Mae swore me to secrecy when she finally told us the truth. Elsie and Harry were there too. I crossed my fingers behind my back when I promised because I don't think there should be secrets between sisters. She said that Mother can never know. I think that is true."

"Who knows?"

"Well, Grace of course. Then Mae, Elsie, you and me. I think we should tell the others. And, Tess, I don't think the baby was stillborn."

"What are you thinking, Hazel?"

"You don't carry a baby nine months and then have a

stillborn child. You would know long before the nine months that the baby was dead. Grace did something with that baby, and I'm thinking it wasn't good."

*****

CHAPTER FOUR

Young Lyman

A few years later, Grace was working at Hartford Hospital and living with three other nurses just near the hospital. Ruth had completed business school, decided it was not for her, and went to Willimantic Normal School where she became a teacher. In the summer of 1924 she was getting ready to start her first teaching job in Cos Cob, Connecticut, in the Fall. Helen was a housewife to her husband, Frank Gage in New Canaan, Connecticut; Florence was the mother to John, Leslie, Howard and Christine Fitts and resided in Eagleville, Connecticut with husband, Fred. Maria and her husband, Egbert Bull, had Betty and Helen; Elsie and Harry had Althea and Lucille; and Kate and D.G. had Leland, Doad, Carol and Donna Reynolds. Lyman was still living at home; Ruth was living with Tess and Bill Peck prior to her departure for Cos Cob; Tess was teaching in the Bill Hill Schoolhouse. Hazel was housewife to Clarence Lee; and Mae to Frank Jones. Sadly, Lyman the elder had passed away from a heart attack the previous summer and Nora lived at the farmhouse with son, Lyman.

The summer started as a hot one and farmers had to use extra care to see that the stock had ample water. Lyman had been running the farm since his father's death and he had not had time for any social life, much less girlfriends. Dorothy had gone by the wayside, with another gentleman from Lyme. Lyman worked very hard to cultivate the fields and to maintain the health of the livestock. Nora helped as much as she could.

It was the beginning of June when Lyman came in early from the fields and he was clutching his side.

He told his mother that he was having some pains and he needed to rest for a while. She prepared a hot water bottle for him to hold on his side and made him comfortable on his bed. The pains grew worse through the later evening and night and Lyman obviously was feverish. Nora called Grace to ask what she could do. Grace told her to keep giving him the hot water bottle for the pain and she would come home the next day to see what she could do. In the meantime she said that if the pain was worse, Nora should call Doctor Ely.

The night was insufferable for Lyman and in the morning Nora called Doc Ely. He said he would come as soon as he could. Nora called Hazel, Tess and Ruth to come to help with the farm chores as Lyman was worried about the stock. They came soon after she called them. When Doc Ely arrived, he examined Lyman, and said that he thought that he was possibly having an appendicitis attack and that it would require surgery as soon as they could get him to the hospital, in this case, to New London. Hazel called Clarence to come and drive him to the hospital in Lyman and Nora's car, acquired just before Lyman's death in 1923.

Nora was sitting by the bed when Clarence arrived to help get Lyman down the stairs and out to the car. Nora held Lyman's hand, "Son, you need to help us get you to the car. You need to go to the hospital."

Lyman looked into her eyes and said "I can't do it,

Mother, I just can't. I love you." He closed his eyes and he was gone.

Ruth gasped and ran shrieking from the room.

"My brother!" She screamed. "My brother is dead! How could this happen? She looked to the sky. "What a cruel God you are! You have taken my brother?"

Her sobbing was not the only crying that was heard from the house. Clarence walked out silently to the telephone and dialed Doc Ely. "We think he is gone," he told him. "He is not breathing."

Doc Ely immediately drove to the farmhouse and took the stairs two at a time up to Lyman's room. Nora was still sitting by the bed, holding Lyman's hand, tears rolling down her cheeks. Doc listened to Lyman's chest with his stethoscope and he shook his head. "He is gone, Nora, I am so sorry. His appendix must have burst."

"But he is only 24," Nora said quietly.

Clarence then called Mr. Jewett to come to take the body. Hazel made the telephone calls to the sisters except for Grace who was already on her way. Tess and Ruth got busy in the kitchen making tea and baking cookies. They needed to be busy. Mae and Maria had arrived from Ivoryton by that time and they sat with

Nora in the parlor, holding her hand. "He was only 24 years old," she said.

"We know, Mother. It just isn't right. It isn't fair. It is just so sad!"

Grace arrived a short time later and was stunned to hear of her brother's death. "I should have come last night," she said, "Maybe I could have helped!"

Nora looked at her. "It isn't your fault, Grace. We all did what we could. He was too sick."

*****

Three days later the Harding Family assembled at the First Congregational Church of Lyme for funeral services for young Lyman. Many townspeople attended as well out of respect for the Hardings. All of the Harding girls were there, with spouses where appropriate, but the young children stayed at home. The girls were bleary-eyed with tears, and they accepted condolences through their grieving. Perhaps the sister closest to Lyman was Ruth. He had been born when Ruth was three, and they had been very close as they grew up together.

Grace surveyed the family as they stood in the condolence line, and she could not help but think that she had suffered the most losses of all of them. Of course no one but Mae knew about the baby, but she still felt a sense of loss. Ruth was acting like the chief mourner, more so than her mother, and Grace thought that was a bit extreme. Perhaps it was her medical training that made her more accepting of illness and death, and she felt bad that Lyman had died, but she wasn't going to be one to wear her emotions on her sleeve.

Tess and Helen were holding Ruth between them, and trying to encourage her. It was time for the family to process up the stairs and into the worship area of the church. Tess and Helen continued to stay close to Ruth as they ascended the stairs. "I can't do this!" Ruth whispered. "I can't go through this."

Tess whispered back, "Just sit there and don't listen. That way you can have your own thoughts and think of Lyman in your own way. It is too hard to listen to others talk about him, especially when we are the ones who knew him the best."

"I am the one who knew him the best," Ruth whispered. "We were the closest. We shared our childhood, our teens and our adulthood. We had a special bond."

Helen said, "Ruth that is true. You and Lyman were especially close. This is a terrible loss for all of us, but particularly for you. I understand that."

The family filed in behind Nora who was escorted by Florence, the eldest. The family filled two pews in the front of the church. The Reverend Val Sundt preceded the family and waited at the altar for all to be seated.

There was an opening prayer, a responsive reading, and then the pastor began his eulogy. "A fine young member of the Lyme community has been taken by our Lord to serve his days in Heaven. We never know what the Lord's reasoning is, but we do know that there is purpose in His choices. Lyman was a good son and brother, as well as a cherished uncle. He was the only son of Lyman and Nora Harding, and upon the elder Lyman's death a year ago, young Lyman took over the role of his father and made the major responsibilities of the farm his own. His sisters were always available to help when they could, while balancing marriages and careers. Lyman never asked for help, but it came to him because he was so loved. His ten sisters and his mother, Nora, adored him. When I asked Nora what she loved best about Lyman, she said it was his smile. She said he was always good-natured, and he was willing to do anything anyone asked of him. We know that Lyman loved his Mother and his sisters in return, and he was never reluctant to express that caring with a hug or two."

As he talked, Ruth wept into her handkerchief. The other sisters were more composed, as was Nora, but it was evident that this loss had hit them very hard with grief. After all, Lyman was only 24 years old.

*****

After the church service, the family walked to the cemetery plot of the Harding family. The cemetery was located directly behind the church. Already interred there were Lyman Darius Harding, the patriarch, and his young son, Lyman Noah Harding, who was born in 1896 and lived only three days. Now Lyman Darius would join them.

The pastor said a prayer as the family surrounded Lyman's casket. Then each one touched the casket as they following their mother's lead, and left the cemetery one by one. Ruth was still weeping.

After they left, the Jewett funeral home men lowered the casket into the ground and filled in the dirt.

Ruth looked back as she passed out the cemetery gates, "Good-bye my love," she whispered.

Everyone gathered at Nora's home and tea was served. The neighbors came to pay their respects as did friends of Lyman. Ruth was exhausted and sat near Nora in the living room. Grace embraced the role of the baby sister quite well, and talked about how much she had looked up to her big brother. In reality she was still thinking about her losses and the fact that everyone did not know how much she had suffered. "Now both my mother and I have lost a child," she thought, forgetting that Nora had also lost a baby long ago. "We both know what it is to lose one of your own."

Maria said, "I feel terribly for Mother. The pain she must feel – losing a child."

Hazel answered. "Yes, losing a child must be very difficult." She looked directly at Grace.

Maria asked, "Does Ruth still plan to take the job in Cos Cob?"

Hazel replied, "Yes but I am worried about her."

"No you aren't," said Grace. You just want to talk about her behind her back." Grace walked across the room to Nora and Ruth. "Can I get you anything?"

Nora shook her head no. Grace turned to Ruth. "Ruth, are you okay? We are worried about you."

Ruth looked at her hands clasped firmly in her lap. "I didn't know how much this could hurt. First Father, then Lyman. It makes you wonder if it is even worth loving someone if it is going to be taken away."

CHAPTER FIVE

Nora continued to live in the Harding house on Sterling City Road, but she sold the stock and tended the garden with the help of some of the girls. Nora lived another 14 years after young Lyman's death, and fortunately did not experience the death of any more of her children.

At this time, Hazel and Clarence lived less than a mile down the road toward Tiffany Farms. Helen, having lost her husband, Frank Gage, married Welles Hallock Martin in 1931 and moved into the Martin Boarding House on Sterling City Road near the church. Since Kate lived at the end of Sterling City Road, and Tess just a few miles down Route 156 at Early Dawn Farm, Nora had 4 daughters living in close proximity to her.

Nora was glad to have Helen back in her life as Helen had been living in New Canaan with Frank. Nora liked Hal Martin and felt he was a good match for Helen. Hal's mother had run the boarding house since the early 1900's and it was often filled with hunters who came to seek the herds of deer that populated the area. By the time that Helen came to live there with Hal, his mother had died and the boarders were few and far between. But Helen did cook for those who came. She had a huge Franklin stove that was powered by wood and she was an excellent cook. When the Lyme Consolidated School opened, several teachers lived at the boarding house. With farming revenue from Hal's work and the boarding fees raised at the house, Helen and Hal lived sparsely but comfortably.

In June of 1934, Grace was attending a church supper with her sisters and mother. She was helping to serve the dinner and she noticed a young man coming through the line whom she had not met. "Hello," she said as he came to her portion of the dinner, "I don't believe we have met. I am Grace Harding."

The young man, who seemed to be alone, smiled. "Nice to meet you, Grace. I am Al Hendry."

Grace took an immediate like to the gentleman and said, "Perhaps we can visit over coffee when I finish my shift."

"That would be very nice," Al said. "I look forward to it!"

Once the main dinner had been served, Grace went to find Al, amiably chatting with the Cone family. There was an empty chair next to him and she slid into it. Grace knew the Cones well; they lived next to Tiffany Farms in Lyme. "There you are!" Al exclaimed. "Time to relax over coffee and dessert! May I get you some pie?"

"Apple, please." Grace answered.

Al went to get the pieces of pie and one of the Stark girls came by to serve coffee. When he returned, he smiled at Grace as he sat down. "So tell me your story, Grace Harding."

Grace blushed. "Well, it looks as if you are new to the area so you probably have not heard of my family. We live here on Sterling City Road and there are ten of us sisters. Our brother died a short time ago of a burst appendix. Most all of my sisters are married and several have children. I am the youngest. I am a nurse."

"Ten girls in one family! Oh my! Your father must have had a time with that!" he chuckled.

"Oh yes he did. We lost my father a few years ago but my mother still keeps an eye on all of us! But tell me about you Al. How did you happen to come to Lyme?"

"Well, I am originally from England, and I still have family there. I came to New York to, you might say, seek my fortune. I did not find work in the city and I found it expensive to live there so I made my way into Connecticut. I found a job as a toll taker on the Baldwin Bridge."

"So you are by yourself? Where do you live?"

"I just found a room in the Martin Boarding House here in Lyme."

"I don't believe it! My sister Helen and her husband Hal own the boarding house. She didn't tell me she had a dapper young man living there!"

"I just moved in today and she told me about this supper. It sounded like a place I could meet people and so I decided to try it out. And look who I met!"

Grace blushed again.

"Are there more of your sisters here?"

"Well, Mother is over at the table by the window with Hazel and her husband, Clarence, and Tess and her husband Bill. Kate is sitting near the children's table where her four little ones are eating. Hazel' s son, Bob, is at the children's table too. Of course Helen is here in the kitchen, but you have met her. Would you like to meet them?"

"I certainly would." Grace beamed. He was such a gentleman and good looking too! It had been a while since Grace and Reg had broken off their relationship and Grace had not dated anyone since. This had been a surprise to the townspeople because the young folks were sure that Grace and Reg would marry and actually gave them a tinware shower. Grace and Reg were very surprised by the shower as they had made no mention of engagement, much less marriage!

"Let's start with Mother," she said. They moved toward the window where the group was sitting. "Mother, I would like you to meet Al Hendry. He is living at Helen's boarding house and is new to town. He is a toll taker on the bridge!"

Nora looked up at Al and offered her hand. "How nice to meet you, Al, Welcome to Lyme!"

Al smiled as he took her hand, "Nice to meet you Mrs. Harding. I have certainly enjoyed meeting your daughter this evening."

Grace introduced Hazel and Clarence, Tess and Bill. Hazel chimed in. "So you work on the bridge, Al. I dare say your accent tells me you are not originally from this area."

"No, I am actually from England. I have been in the United States for three months and am hoping to make it my home."

"England! That is so far away! How long a trip was it to get here?" Tess asked.

"It took a little over a month to get here. Definitely an interesting experience. When we have more time someday I will tell you about the journey."

Grace took his arm. "Come and meet Kate."

Kate smiled as they approached. "Kate, this is Al Hendry. He is new to the area and works on the bridge."

"Nice to meet you," Al and Kate said in unison and then laughed. "These are my children," Kate pointed, "Leland, Doad, Carol and Donna. And this young man is our nephew, Bob."

"That's quite a handful you have there, Kate," Al smiled. "Hello children."

"Say hello to Mr. Hendry, children," Kate admonished.

"Hello Mr. Hendry!"

Grace was ready to have Al to herself so she suggested that they take a walk in the evening air. He readily agreed.

As they walked along Sterling City Road and past the boarding house toward Sterling City itself, Grace talked about her other sisters and their lives as well. Al told her about his family and how much he missed them, but that he thought he would have a good life in

America. When they came to the Harding homestead, Grace invited him to sit on the porch and visit. They talked easily for another hour, during which time Nora came home and, after greeting them both, went in to bed. She smiled to herself as she went into the house, "Grace has a beau!" she thought.

*****

In September of 1934, Grace accepted Al Hendry's proposal of marriage and they moved to Sterling City Road in a house owned by Tess between Hazel's and the Harding homestead.

Mae and Frank continued their regular Sunday visits to Nora, Hazel, Helen, Kate, Grace and Tess. Elsie and Harry came every other Sunday, and Ruth came home on some week-ends to see the family. Maria and Egbert came to visit on Saturdays with Betty and Helen from Ivoryton. Florence was not as attentive as the others, and was busy with her own family in Eagleville. They would all come for Thanksgiving and Christmas.

Florence

Fitts Children

Life went on as usual and Nora's grandchildren were precious to her. She delighted in the days that the girls visited with their children. She had thirteen grandchildren, five boys and eight girls. Their births started with Mabel Fitts in 1908 and extended to 1925 with Bob Lee. When the children were at the Harding homestead they loved playing as cousins, and especially liked going into the barn and climbing into the haylofts. They played hide and seek and there were incredible places to hide. Their mothers took them skating on the adjacent Mill Pond in the winter; something they had grown up doing in the late 1800's and early 1900's. Nora loved to have them visit in the parlor where they were very well behaved. It was assumed that their mothers had taught them that it was appropriate to show respect for their grandmother by sitting politely and answering any questions she asked. Needless to say, they were not always so well-behaved at other times!

In October 1934 Mae and Frank, Elsie and Harry made their usual Sunday visit to see Nora, the first stop on their usual rounds. They sat in the parlor and Nora asked, "Well what is going on in your lives this week?"

Mae was excited, "Frank is putting together a bulletin board at the store of all the men and boys who are going into the service. The families have given him pictures!"

Nora, coughing a bit, said "What a nice gesture, Frank."

Elsie reported that Lucille and Althea were with Harry's parents for a week-end at the beach.

"What fun for them!" Nora answered.

Mae asked Nora, "What about you, Mother? What do you know?"

"Well, Ruth is very busy now that she has become an assistant principal in Cos Cob. She barely has time to come home. I see all of the other girls though. Except Florence. She and her family stay pretty close to their home. I always wondered why she was so independent."

Mae answered. "Well she is the oldest. She does live pretty far away."

"You seem a bit low today, Mother. Is everything okay?"

"Oh I am just tired," Nora said. No reason but I just feel worn out. Maybe being 77 is catching up with me."

Elsie suggested, "Perhaps it is the weather. It has been so up and down lately."

Mae asked, "Do you feel like lying down, Mother? We can move on to Helen's if you want to take a rest."

"Maybe that would be good. Give the other girls my best."

*****

Upon arriving at Helen and Hal's, the girls expressed their concern about Nora. Helen said "I talked with her this morning and I knew something wasn't right. She seemed very slow in responding. We should have Grace check her out."

Elsie said "Good idea. Let's call Grace now."

After the call Grace went immediately to see Nora. Grace called Helen. "I am going to call Doc Ely.

Mother is having some shortness of breath and says she is very tired. I think you should come over here."

"Okay I will be there right away." She turned to the others. "Grace is calling Doc Ely. I am going over. I don't think we need everyone there right now. Why don't you go along with your visiting and put the others on alert. Then we know everyone is aware that she is having some problems."

When Helen arrived, Doc Ely was pulling in to the driveway. He went directly to Nora's room. After about 10 minutes he came out.

"She is having some breathing difficulties and I think her lungs are congested. I have a tonic that I want you to give her every three hours. And keep her in bed. She does have a slight fever. Can you organize your sisters so that someone is always sitting with her?"

Helen replied. "I will get on that immediately."

Despite expert care from Doc Ely and Grace, Nora passed away within weeks. Once again the family assembled for a funeral, and proceeded as they had in the past. This time it was more expected as Nora was 77 years old. All the sisters were there and all the grandchildren as well. There were four pews of Hardings in the church. Nora was laid to rest in the Harding plot next to her husband.

It was then time to sell the Harding homestead. Grace took the lead with Ruth in an advising role because, after all, she had a business background. It took some time to clean out the home where there were years and years of memories, and the sisters came to take anything that belonged to them. After a year, the home sold to a young farmer and his wife, who were anxious to start a business and a family. The sisters divided the money received for the home equally. Grace did feel she should receive more as she had done the majority of the work.

Ruth was then serving as an assistant principal in Cos Cob. The combination of business and education made her a good candidate for the administrative position and she was enjoying her career. When she did come to Lyme to visit, she stayed with Tess and Bill. She was really the only one who had branched out very far from the Harding ties. When asked if she missed being close to the family, she responded. "I am an independent career woman. I love my family and I see them often. My work is very rewarding to me. To make a difference in the lives of children is an opportunity that not everyone has."

The sisters did not worry about Ruth as she was perceived as strong-willed and intelligent. She would be successful in her chosen path.

CHAPTER SIX

Maria

Perhaps the one sister who was most distressed about Nora's death was Maria. When she married Egbert Bull in 1918 she had moved immediately "across the river" to Ivoryton where Egbert had his family home. Maria had been extremely close to her mother and father and she felt a sense of abandoning them when she moved with Egbert. But it was natural to be with her husband, and, after two miscarriages, she gave birth to Elizebeth Harding Bull, soon to be called

Betsy and eventually Betty, in December of 1921. Betsy was a happy and easy baby, healthy and robust. Both Maria and Egbert were delighted with their little girl. Egbert was a banker at the Essex Savings Bank and made a decent living. Maria was free to concentrate on raising Betsy and her days were filled with the fun and love that childcare brought. Nora and Lyman adored Betsy and could not get enough of her when the Bulls visited on Saturdays. They had special time then, because they saw the others mostly on Sundays.

When Betsy was two-and-a-half, her sister, Helen, was born. She was a small baby and in contrast to Betsy she was sickly and fussy. She was a pretty baby, but her temperament was not as positive. Betsy was thrilled to have a "baby" in the house and paid lots of attention to Helen. Even though she was a harder child to deal with than Betsy, Maria loved her second daughter just as much.

Betsy and Helen

The girls grew up in the Bull house in Ivoryton. As they grew older they could walk to Frank Jones' store where he would treat them to candy sticks. They went to elementary school in Ivoryton and both did well in school. Betsy said that when she grew up she wanted to be a teacher, and Helen said she wanted to be a person in a business, whatever that meant to her.

One day Maria and the children were in the car waiting outside the bank for Egbert. The girls were then 12 and 9 years old. They were watching out the windows at the cars going by and waving to people on the streets. A car just like theirs went by, driven by a man similar to Egbert's size. Maria blurted out, "Oh no! Your father forgot us! There he goes without us!" She quickly realized her error and blushed. The children giggled in the back seat. Egbert then came out of the bank, got into the car, and they were off to do their errands.

Betsy and Helen loved visiting the Harding homestead, especially when there were a lot of their cousins there. Betsy was best friends with her cousin Donna Reynolds; Donna was a year older than Betsy. Helen liked Bob the best. He was always willing to try things that maybe they shouldn't do, such as climb the highest tree, or swim farther out into the cove than others.

Egbert had been in banking since his marriage to Maria. He was good at his job and he loved working at the Essex Savings Bank. He had a good way with people. Around 1935, he began suffering from extreme headaches. He saw Doctor Young in Ivoryton who said that he had too much stress in his job, and being 41 years old, he should not have such reactions unless he was over-stressed. Doc Young prescribed aspirin and early to bed nights for Egbert. For a while this regimen helped, but as time went on, Egbert found himself tiring easily and sometimes having trouble focusing his eyes. The headaches had returned. After a year, Egbert could no longer work as he was so ill. He became bedridden. Maria, feeling a bit weak herself, found it difficult to care for Egbert and to help Betsy and Helen, although they were 16 and 13 at the time. The girls missed the visits to Lyme but they understood. The sisters did come to see Maria but they did not bring the cousins as it would be too much for Egbert. They worried about Maria as well; she was pale and seemed to be extremely tired. They always brought food when they came so Maria would not have to cook.

Maria, Betsy, Helen, Egbert

Betty, Helen and Maria entered Frank's store. Betty smiled, "Hi Uncle Frank!"

"Well hello ladies! What brings you by today?"

Maria spoke up. "Egbert needed some quiet time and we decided we could use some fresh air so we walked here."

Frank asked, "Is he still having those headaches?"

"Didn't Mae tell you?"

"Tell me what?"

"Doc says it is a brain tumor."

Frank was astounded. "No! Can it be treated?"

"No," Maria hung her head.

"This must be so hard. Do they know?" Frank looked over at the girls who were looking at the candy supply.

"Yes, I have told them. I am hoping they won' t take it so hard when it happens."

"What do you mean?"

"Well, look at Ruth. After Lyman died she said she didn't want to get married or have kids. It is like she is afraid to get close to anyone. I don't want that for my girls."

"They won't react like Ruth did. How are you doing?"

"The love of my life is dying."

"If Mae or I can do anything please let us know."

"Thanks, we will."

*****

In October 1937, precisely two years after the initial headaches began, Maria was sitting in the bedroom with Egbert, doing her needlepoint as he slept. The girls had gone to bed. Egbert opened his eyes and looked at Maria; she smiled at him and took his hand. "Come with me, Maria!" He whispered with some excitement in his voice. "Come with me in the tunnel. I see the bright light where we must go. I love you and I want you with me." As he closed his eyes for the last time, Maria said softly, "The children, Egbert, I must stay for the children." And he was gone.

Maria felt pains in her heart, and she clutched at it as she bent forward to cry out in anguish. Her husband was gone, she was not well, and she had two children who needed their parents. She cried for the loss of Egbert, the loss of her mother and father, the loss of Lyman, and she cried for herself, in pain and alone.

She waited until morning to talk to the children about their father. Both girls cried when they heard that he was dead. Betsy said "But we didn't have a chance to say good-bye. We couldn't tell him we loved him!"

"You both showed him every day how much you loved him," Maria said. "And he loved you so much. You made him very proud."

The family gathered for a graveside service at the cemetery in Ivoryton where Egbert was laid to rest in the Bull plot, alongside his mother and father. There would be room there for Maria as well. All the sisters were there, as well as the nieces and nephews. Everyone went back to the Bull house after the service. Each sister had brought something for a potluck supper and the family visited quietly over their meal.

Helen asked Maria, "What will you do now, Maria? Will you go to work?"

"I guess I will have to find something that I can do," she answered. But she looked so frail that the sisters could not believe that she would be able to. Perhaps after some time passed she would be able to gain strength and go to work to support her children. "We have some savings that will help for a while," she added.

Grace, ever the in-charge sister, chimed in. "Betsy is old enough to go to work. Maybe you could hire her at the store, Frank?" Frank looked up with surprise at the mention of his name.

"Huh?"

"Betsy could work for you to help support the family, couldn't she? You could take some time off and enjoy life!"

"Well I have never had any help with the store. Mae comes in sometimes but it is not necessary."

"Well," Grace said, "It certainly seems that you could help your sister-in-law out by hiring Betsy. Helen is still too young, but Betsy could be a big help."

The children were all in another room and did not hear this discussion.

Grace scoffed at Frank. He gave her a long gaze.

Maria said, "If Betsy works, the money she earns should go toward her tuition to become a teacher. Her priority right now is to do well in school and work toward her goals. I will manage to support my family."

Grace said, "Come on Al, time for us to be headed back to Lyme." Al obediently arose and headed toward the door. Eventually the sisters and their families left, hugging Maria and the girls and promising to get together soon.

After a week, Maria asked Frank to teach her to drive the car. She knew she would need to be able to transport the girls, do her grocery shopping and go to appointments. He agreed to do that on the next Sunday morning before church and visiting. The store was closed on Sundays.

Maria was a quick learner and she felt confident behind the wheel. She had Betsy go on the lesson too so she could also start to drive. It would be important that they both learn. Frank was very patient and it helped that his pupils were confident.

It was fortuitous that Maria had insisted on this because instead of growing stronger after Egbert died, Maria grew weaker. Doc Young said there was a problem with her heart and that she had to be careful about not pushing herself too hard. He prescribed an aspirin a day and significant bouts of rest. Maria never did pursue getting a job, but supported her girls on the savings that Egbert had accumulated for them. He had been a smart man. She tried very hard not to show that she was feeling poorly, and she spent a lot of time with the girls.

Betsy and Helen watched as their mother grew weaker and they made sure they were quiet and good so that she did not have to worry. Frank did make arrangements for Betsy to work at the store after school, but he did not leave and take any breaks. Betsy saved her money in an old cigar box in her dresser drawer. "Someday I will be able to go to school to be a teacher," she thought. "And I will be a wonderful teacher!"

As it became noticeable that Maria was becoming weaker, Doc Young suggested that she have her sisters take in the girls for a while so she could rest. "I will not split up my family," she declared.

Just six months after Egbert's death, Maria 's heart gave out and she died in her sleep. Betsy found her in her bed in the morning, and she called Frank. Frank came over and called Doc Young who came and pronounced her dead. Betsy and Helen stood by the bed in shock. They knew that she had been ill, but they had not expected this. When the funeral director came to take Maria's body away, the girls sobbed in the parlor. By then Mae was there, along with Grace and Tess.

Mae asked the sisters, "What shall we do with the girls? They can't stay here alone."

Grace stepped in. "We will need to decide among us who is best able to care for both or one. In the meantime, Mae, you could have them with you temporarily and they would still be able to go to their schools."

"Oh! Well, yes." Mae said, somewhat surprised but always willing to do as she was told.

Tess went into the parlor. "Betsy, Helen, I want you to pack a few days of clothes. You are going to stay with Mae and Frank while we all decide what is best for you for living arrangements."

The girls looked at her. "We can stay here," Helen said. "Betsy and I know how to cook and we can take care of ourselves."

"No," Tess replied. Your aunts will decide what is best for you. Go now and pack up."

The girls walked slowly toward the stairs to go to their bedrooms. "But what if we don't like what you decide?" Helen said, with an edge to her voice.

Grace responded. "It is not for you to like it or not. It is what we are willing to do to help you out. And we will decide that ourselves. This is what your mother would have wanted. Go!"

The graveside service was similar to that for Egbert and Betsy and Helen held roses that they placed on their mother's casket. The whole family was there and afterwards everyone gathered at Mae and Frank's house. Helen and Betsy had been staying upstairs where they shared a bed. They liked being close at this time, and they didn't ever want to give Mae a hard time. She was so sweet.

Apparently the sisters had been talking about what

was best for the girls and they had decided that Helen would stay with Mae and Betsy would go with Helen and Hal in Lyme. Once again, Grace decided it was her responsibility to impart the news.

"But for how long?" Helen was crying at the thought of being separated from Betsy.

"As long as needed," Grace answered. "You should be grateful that your aunts are willing to change their lives to take care of orphans like you are."

Betsy choked back tears. "Orphans! What a horrible thing to say! It may be true but it still isn't nice of you to say!"

"You will be well cared for, and you will behave yourselves in gratitude for being given such nice, kind homes," Grace spat.

"Well at least we don't have to live with YOU!" Helen said and ran upstairs to the bedroom.

Hazel spoke to Grace, "Well you certainly made a mess of that! The poor girls have lost mother and father within six months of each other, and you come on like some tyrant. Calling them orphans…they won't be in any orphanage. We will all see to that!"

Grace spoke back, "I didn't see you stepping forward to help out. Of course you have your precious Bob to care for. I suppose another child would be too much for you!"

"As a matter of fact, I would take either one of them. I just don't have room for both of them right now. " Hazel huffed.

Everyone milled around and discussed what should be done with the Bull house and its contents. The children were taken care of according to their plans so there would have to be a sale and the money would be set up in accounts for the girls. One by one the families left and headed to their respective homes, Betsy in the car with Helen and Hal. Young Helen lay on the bed and cried herself to sleep, missing Betsy.

"Someday I will see that Grace regrets being so mean to us," Helen said to herself. "I will be sure that she gets what she deserves."

*****

When Betsy arrived in Lyme with Helen and Hal, Helen said "Let us know if you need anything."

"Thank you, Helen."

"I am really sorry about your parents. We are all grieving with you."

"I know."

"Hal said he will drive you across the river everyday so you can go to your school."

Betsy brightened. "He will?"

"Yes. Now get washed up. We will have a little supper."

CHAPTER SEVEN

Betsy

Betsy settled in to her room at the back of Helen and Hal's house. Her room overlooked the back pasture and the Tighe place next door. Marvel Tighe and her mother, Mrs. Kindly, lived in the small white house with the one car garage and the beautiful lilac bushes. Right behind and next to their house were the fairgrounds where the Hamburg Fair was held on the third Saturday of every August. It was one of Betsy's favorite days.

Betsy had worried about school but Hal assured her he would drive her across the river to finish her schooling at Pratt High School. She had two years to go. She was glad because her best friend Tinker still lived in Ivoryton and this would be the only way she would get to see her, at school. She gave Hal a big hug when he said he would take her. She missed having young Helen around, but she adjusted quickly to living on Sterling City Road, attending church each Sunday with her cousins. She and Donna always sat together in church and were in the same Sunday School class. At that time children attended Sunday School through age 18, and the 17 and 18-year-olds actually helped out with the younger children's lessons.

Betsy grew to know her aunts even more as the Lyme group tended to spend a lot of time together. She learned to sew from Helen, and she became quite good at using the Singer Sewing Machine in Helen's living room. She helped clean the rooms of the boarders, although there were not many, and she enjoyed hearing the stories told at the dinner table. She always helped with the dishes and then did her homework.

Hal had cows and chickens and Betsy loved to go to the barn to help him milk the cows. She also liked collecting the warm brown eggs that the chickens laid in the hen house. It was a different life from the one she had in Ivoryton, but she liked it. She saw Helen every Sunday when Frank and Mae made their rounds. Helen told her that it was nice at the Jones house but she was bored without Betsy. Helen did not have many friends, and school was not her favorite place to be. But she was doing well and she said she was being good.

When Helen was 15, she began seeing a boy named Roger Daunting. Roger's family was from Essex, Connecticut, and he attended Pratt High School with Helen. Betsy was a senior there and Helen was finishing her freshman year. Helen really liked Roger and she started spending a great deal of time with him away from Frank and Mae's house. Mae asked that she please let her know where she was going but Helen always said "Out." And Mae, being the innocent and sweet sister, let it go.

After several months of Helen's being away most of the time, but coming home for dinner, homework and bed, Mae mentioned to Tess that she was concerned that Roger was taking up too much of Helen's time and that she needed to do other things, one of which was some chores at home. Tess decided to share the news with Ruth, Hazel and Grace, as they had been the main decision-makers on where the girls should live.

Tess called Ruth, and Hazel and Grace came on the line since they were all on the same party line. The conversation was intense.

"What is she doing all the time with this boy?" Grace asked.

Tess answered. "Mae doesn't know because Helen won't tell her where she is going or how long she will be gone. She just says she is going out. She doesn't seem to have time for her chores."

Ruth chimed in. "And you say Helen is not helping with the chores?"

Grace chimed in. "What an ungrateful child!"

"I think it is good that she has found a boyfriend," Hazel said.

"Good? When it takes her away from doing what she should? When she spends almost all of her waking hours with him? This girl needs to be whipped into shape!" Grace exclaimed. "I know, Tess, you take her for a while. You have Ruth's room when she is not there and, when she is, Helen can sleep on the couch in the parlor. It is time she learned some discipline."

"Why me?" Tess exclaimed.

"Because you can teach her the frugal, farming life. She can spend her time milking those cows rather than fooling around with some boy. She can go to the Old Lyme School instead of Pratt. That should stop all this nonsense."

"I think you are over-reacting" Hazel said. "She just needs some boundaries set and Mae isn't strong enough to set them. What if we all sit down with Helen and tell her our concerns?"

"It has already gone too far, Hazel." Grace answered, sneering. "I say we move the girl to the Early Dawn Farm and knock some sense into her."

Grace called Mae and told her the plan. She and Al would come over that evening, have Helen pack, and they would take her to Tess. She told Mae there would be no arguments and Helen would just have to adjust. Mae sighed and said she felt that she had failed. "You didn't fail, Mae, Helen did. Maria would never stand for her behavior like this."

That evening Grace and Al pulled into the Jones' driveway. Helen, Mae and Frank were just finishing dinner. Helen had noticed that Mae wasn't eating much and appeared nervous. When Grace and Al came in, Helen was taken aback. "Helen," Grace said, "We have had a change in plans. We want you to go upstairs and pack your things. You are moving to Lyme to live with Tess and Bill."

"What? What do you mean moving?" Helen was shocked.

"You can't behave here and follow the rules. You haven't been doing your chores and you have been fooling around with some boy. All of that must stop. You are moving. End of story."

Helen looked at Mae. "Mae – you didn't say anything about this. You didn't ask me to do more chores. You let me go with Roger. Why don't you want me anymore?"

Mae started, "Helen, it's not that I don't…"

Grace interrupted. "Go upstairs and pack your things NOW. You have fifteen minutes or we go without them!"

Helen leered at Grace. "You have always hated me. You just want to make my life miserable. It is not fair! I love Roger!" She stormed off.

Mae started to cry. Grace stiffened. Frank stared at his coffee cup and Al twisted his hat in his hands. "Stop it, Mae," Grace said, "Helen always has been a difficult child and we are just not going to stand for it. Get yourself together!"

Mae answered. "You are NOT her mother!"

"Neither are you." Grace lashed out. "You are NO ONE'S mother!" Mae sobbed harder.

Helen came back downstairs with two bags. "Is that everything?" Grace asked. Helen stared at her and walked out the door. "No thank you to Mae and Frank for keeping you?" Helen kept walking toward the car.

Helen got in the back seat with her bags. Grace and Al said good-bye to Mae and Frank and hustled to the car.

Grace turned to Helen in the back seat. "I'll tell you what, young lady, you better shape up and get rid of that attitude pretty darn fast. You may end up being a ward of the State and living under their care in some orphanage. Is that what you want?" Helen said nothing.

When they arrived at the Early Dawn Farm it was 7 P.M. Tess welcomed Helen, but Helen simply walked past her, mumbling "Where do I take my bags?"

"Upstairs to the right, Helen. That will be your room when Ruth is away."

Helen started up the stairs and then turned back, looking at Tess. "I have homework to do so I won't be back down until time for school tomorrow."

Grace called out, "You may as well not waste your time on your homework. You will start a new school, Old Lyme, tomorrow."

"WHAT?" Helen raised her voice. I can still go to Pratt. Call Hal and he will take me when he takes Betsy. He takes her every day to school."

"No," Grace said. "You are changing schools and getting away from that boy." Helen turned and stomped up the rest of the stairs. In a moment the door to her room slammed shut. Tess looked at Grace.

"What am I in for?" she asked.

CHAPTER EIGHT

As soon as she could, Helen went back down the stairs and picked up the telephone in the parlor. Tess and Bill were in the kitchen listening to the radio. She dialed Roger's number and he answered the telephone. She told him what had happened. He told her not to worry, that they would figure something out. He suggested that she call Betsy to see if she could get Hal to pick her up and take her to Pratt the next morning. Her next call was to Betsy and her aunt, Helen, answered the phone.

"Hi, this is Helen," she said quietly. "May I please talk to Betsy?"

Helen had no idea what had happened and assumed that young Helen was calling from Mae's. "Sure, dear, I will call her to the telephone."

Betsy picked up the receiver, "Hi Helen. What's up?"

"I want our old life back. I want Mother and Father

to be alive again and I want to be at the Bull house. I want to live with you again. It is all so horrid!"

Helen told her what had happened and Betsy felt tears filling her eyes. She had always felt responsible for protecting her younger sister but had not been able to do so since her mother's death and the splitting up of the sisters. "Helen, just behave with Tess. Do as you are asked and don't rock the boat. It might be a good place to live anyway."

"But they say I have to go to school in Old Lyme, and that Hal can't take me to Pratt with you."

Betsy replied. "I don't see – oh yeah, they want you away from Roger. I don't think we can get around that one."

Helen answered tearfully, "But he is my boyfriend! I love Roger!"

"You probably think you do. But wait until you meet some of the Old Lyme boys. I'll bet there are some really cute ones."

"I understand, you are upset, but we are not yet of the age that we are allowed to make our own decisions. You must be patient and do as they ask. Remember, it is easier to smile than to frown."

"Maybe for you it is. Right now I don't want any part of this Harding family."

They told each other good night and Helen snuck back up the stairs and cried herself to sleep.

When morning came, Tess called up to her. "Breakfast is ready, and you need to leave for school in 30 minutes! Rise and shine!"

Helen rubbed her eyes and sat up on the bed. She was still in her dress from yesterday and she had not unpacked. She decided she would try to buy some time. When she entered the kitchen she was still wearing yesterday's clothes. "I am really not feeling well, Tess. I don't think I should go to school today."

"Well, other than your wrinkled clothes, you look fine to me." Tess felt her forehead. "No fever. Here, eat your oatmeal and drink your tea. Then get dressed for school."

"But..."

"No 'buts.' This is how today is going to work. You are going to eat, dress and then stand out by the gate where the school bus will pick you up. The bus will bring you home at 3 P.M. I have your lunch all packed. Now get to eating."

Helen did as she was told. She was on time for the bus,

and she felt very strange getting on alone and then she saw that her cousins Donna and Carol were on the bus. She felt a little better then. Donna and Carol asked what she was doing there. She explained that she had moved in with Tess and Bill and would be attending school in Old Lyme. Donna asked if Betsy was coming too and Helen said no, that Helen and Hal were honoring her wishes to still attend Pratt. She decided not to get into the fact that she wanted to go to Pratt as well.

When they arrived at the school, Donna took her to the office so she could find out about her classes. Helen met with a secretary who matched up the courses with those she had been taking at Pratt. Then she walked Helen to her first class.

In the meantime, Betsy was a senior at Pratt and was getting ready to apply to Willimantic State Teacher's College. She had the grades for it and she had worked hard. She was dating William Ackerman, a boy from Ivoryton who lived near the Ivoryton Playhouse and worked there in the summer season. He was exciting because he had met many famous actors who came there in summer stock. William could drive and he would come to Lyme to take Betty out on dates. She also saw him each day in school. William had decided he wanted to be an actor, but his parents had decided he would become a businessman or banker.

Betsy loved living with Helen and Hal. They treated her so well, and she loved helping out where she could. She was going to miss them when she went away to college; the sale of the Bull house had left her enough money for college and she was grateful for that. She might get a scholarship, but there were not many available.

Helping in the Sunday School had affirmed her love for children and her desire to be an elementary level teacher. Betsy thought she had everything going for her. Although she was dating William at the time, she had noticed that there was a really nice boy at church who was a bit younger than she. She really liked him and talked with him even though he was, at the time, 14 years old and she was 18. His name was Ken Plimpton and he came to church with his 12 year old brother, Allan, and his youngest brother, Howard, who was 7. Ken had a shy way about him but he was comfortable with Betsy and he liked talking with her. So they were Sunday friends.

Helen eventually made the transition to the Old Lyme school and got to know many of the "Lymies" who went there. She, too, had met Ken and Allan Plimpton as well. Ken was on the baseball team and Allan would hang around the practices and games, waiting for him to finish. Then they would walk the five miles home. Helen was adjusting to living with Tess and Bill. Bill hardly talked at all, but Tess was a chatterbox and wanted to know everything that was going on in Helen's life. Helen had not seen nor heard from Roger and so she decided that it might be time to look for a new boyfriend. She did not discuss that plan with Tess as it was the reason that she had to leave Mae's. But Helen willingly helped with the farm chores, learning to milk cows and weed the gardens. She helped with the dishes after supper before she did her homework. All seemed to be working out well for her.

June came and Betsy graduated from Pratt High School. Helen and Hal had a gathering at the house to celebrate. Most of the family came to the party, with the exception of Florence who had not been feeling well. The trip would have been too much for her. Ruth was the proudest aunt there, as Betsy was going to follow in her footsteps and become a teacher. Ruth was still working in Cos Cob and enjoying her role as both assistant principal and teacher. She was considering a job change to Essex for the next year but had not made the commitment just yet.

The summer was a blur for Betsy as she worked at Frank's store, and planned for college. In The Fall of 1939, off she went to Willimantic and met her college roommate, Maureen Dowd. They liked each other instantly and they had fun comparing coursework and teachers. The dormitory was small but comfortable.

College was different because she was really on her

own. There was no one to tell her when to go where or what to do. She had to use self-discipline and guide herself throughout her learning experience. Teachers advised her on the courses she needed and she loved the classroom work.

In December, when she went home for Christmas break, she learned upon arrival that her aunt, Florence, had passed away in her sleep. Florence had been working for a gentleman named W.A. Pierce in Stafford, Connecticut, and had spent that night there due to a winter storm that closed the roads. She left her husband Fred a widower, and their three sons and one daughter, all married. She was the eldest of the Harding children and the first sister to die. She was 56 years old.

The funeral was in Eagleville when Florence and Fred lived. Most of the sisters and spouses made the trip for the gathering. Helen and Hal took Betsy, but most of the younger generation did not go because they did not know the Fitts family well. They tended to show up for Thanksgiving and Christmas when Nora was living, but stopped this practice after her death. Otherwise they had been seen at funerals.

Grace and Al did not attend. Grace said it would be hypocritical to go to mourn a sister who was so much older that she hardly knew her, and who didn't pay much attention to the family anyway. She convinced

Mae and Frank to miss the event as well. The other sisters attended.

Betsy went back to school after the Christmas break and was happy to do so. She loved Helen and Hal, but she loved college too. She was no longer dating William Ackerman, and had met John Elliott, a boy from Willimantic. He was already graduated from a business school and was working as a bookkeeper for an insurance company. They went out dancing on Friday and Saturday nights. Sometimes they played tennis on the week-ends. Betsy really enjoyed his company.

Meanwhile Helen was then in tenth grade at Old Lyme, and loving school. She was not, however, enjoying home life with Tess and Bill. She felt Tess was taking advantage of her with many chores, and one was the most disgusting she had ever done. She had to wash the bathroom rags by hand, hang them on the outside line, bring them in and fold them when dry, and replace them in the bathroom. This was an unnecessary task, she knew, because at school they used toilet paper, not rags. But Tess was too cheap to buy toilet paper. Tess even wanted Helen to use old newspaper as pads when she had her monthly period; Helen used the rags instead. She vowed she would get a job and earn enough money to buy toilet paper and sanitary supplies, such as they were. One of the worst parts of living with Tess and Bill was that baths were taken in an old washtub in the kitchen. Helen longed for privacy.

Helen finally told Tess that she was finished with washing the rags. She told Tess that she was being taken advantage of, and that she was only a 16 year-old girl who needed her time to do homework and make herself look pretty. This did not go over well with Tess. When Tess told her she would continue with her chores as assigned, Helen stormed up the stairs, packed her bags and walked the three miles to Hazel's house. Hazel was surprised to see her on the doorstep.

Clarence and Hazel

"Helen," what are you doing here with your bags?"

"I want to live with you, Clarence and Bob," Helen answered. Bob was then going to the Buckley School in New London instead of to the Old Lyme school. "I don't want to live with Tess anymore."

Hazel brought her in, sat her down at the kitchen table and made her some tea. "What did Tess do?"

"Well, she makes me do awful chores. And she doesn't give me any time to do the things I need to do. She is cheap and she makes me use newspapers for my monthly!"

Hazel knew all too well how cheap Tess was, and she and Clarence had avoided using the bathroom there for years. She knew about the one teabag serving, and she knew that Bill received an allowance when the milk money came in. She was pretty sure that living with Tess was not really an appropriate place for a teenage girl.

"Does Tess know where you are?" Hazel asked.

"No – and I don't really care. She and Grace are mean to me and I don't like them very much. You have always been nice to me, Hazel, and I really like Bob. We have fun together. I will be good, I promise. I know you will be reasonable about my chores and I won't complain. Can I stay here, please?"

Hazel nodded. "Let me call Tess and tell her where you are, as she must be worried. I will tell her we will try you out here for a few weeks and see how it goes." Helen smiled.

Hazel called Tess. She was right, Tess had been frantic, not knowing where Helen was. Tess did not drive and Bill was out working the fields so she couldn't drive along the road to look for Helen. "She's a headstrong one, Hazel. I hope you realize what you are in for."

Ten minutes after hanging up, Hazel was helping Helen settle in to the guest room upstairs, next to Bob's room. He was not home as he was with his father, helping to pick up some supplies he needed for a new house he was building. Hazel's phone rang. She answered and it was Grace. "You have some nerve!" she shouted into the telephone. "What do you think you are doing?"

"Grace, what are you talking about?"

"Letting Helen get away with running from Tess because she doesn't want to help with chores! You never even consulted me!"

"And what business is it or yours?" Hazel asked testily.

"I am the one who decides what to do with Helen. None of you have the guts to deal with this girl. She always gets what she wants. She is just so stubborn that she fights her way into situations where she does not belong. You are too soft for her."

"Grace, I said we would try it for a few weeks. I really don't know why you feel you must be in charge. And I don't see why you are berating me. I am just trying to help. I have as much responsibility to my sister's child as you do."

"Oh yeah, Hazel? You are just too ignorant to know what you are being played for the fool."

"Is that right, Grace? You are so righteous. By the way, what DID happen to that baby you had in nursing school?"

Hazel heard her gasp and then the line went dead. Hazel feared she may have gone a step too far but darn it, Grace had called her ignorant. Grace was always the controlling one, the one who talked behind everyone's back and sweet talked them to their faces, except for her. Grace had never really been nice to her, ever.

As for Helen, she stayed with Hazel, Clarence and Bob until after her graduation from the Old Lyme school in 1942, and then went on to Morse Business College in Hartford. Money from the sale of the Bull home supported Helen in her endeavors. She found a roommate and an apartment and was finally on her own. On completion of her coursework she took a position with the Selective Service Board, a job formerly held by her cousin Donna.

After Betsy graduated from Willimantic State Teacher's College, she found a job teaching first grade in Flanders, Connecticut. She loved the children and her job in the East Lyme area. She lived at home with Helen and Hal as it was close enough to commute each day. She changed her name from Betsy to Betty, as she thought Betsy was more suited for a young child. She became very close to her principal, Jane Renfrew, and to a colleague, Lillie Haynes. Lil and her husband Clarence would be good friends of Betty's and Ken's for years to come.

In 1946 Betty started dating Ken Plimpton, a graduate of Mitchell Junior College in New London, CT. Ken lived at home about two miles north on Route 156 with his father, Kenneth Plimpton Sr., and his brothers Allan and Howard. His mother had died in 1942 and his father had re-married to Fannie Fields, of Essex, CT. Fannie had two daughters, Marie and Marjorie who were close in age to Ken and Allan.

Betty and Ken had a lot in common and loved to ski, skate, shoot 22's, play tennis, and go boating. They also loved archery and had their own bows and arrows for target shooting. Ken had been accepted into the aviation cadet enlisted reserve and was trained as a pilot. He served in the Air Force Reserves from 1944 to

1946 in Biloxi, Mississippi. When Betty started dating him, he had finished his service and was working at the Norwich Finishing Company as a production manager.

Betty and Ken were married in January of 1947. They were married in the First Congregational Church of Lyme and the ceremony was performed by the long time pastor, the Reverent Val Sundt. Only the immediate families were in attendance. Helen and Hal held a reception at the Martin house in celebration of the union. The aunts were all a-buzz about the wedding and were thrilled that Betty was marrying into the Ely family. Ken's mother was Marguerite Ely, daughter of Dr. Josiah Ely, the town physician. The Ely family was as close to royalty as one could get in the town of Lyme, and therefore the sisters regarded the match as one of high prestige.

By this time, Doc Ely's son, Julian, had finished his medical training and was working with his father in the town's medical practice. He would eventually take over the practice and continue to be the town doctor and coroner until he was in his 90's. He and his wife, May Richardson, lived in the Doc Ely house, where the office was always located, and May was quite taken with herself for becoming the wife of the young doctor. They had two boys of their own, Julian II and William Marvin. The boys were in the same age range as their cousins, Allan and Howard Plimpton.

With Clarence's carpentry skills as an assist, Hal put in a second kitchen in the Martin house and Betty and Ken moved in to one half of the house on Sterling City Road. It was like an apartment for them, although the house had only one bathroom that was shared by all. There were no longer many boarders at the house but occasionally a teacher would stay there for the week nights. So they had the kitchen, a living room with fireplace, and two bedrooms upstairs next to the bathroom. Betty continued her teaching job but also helped tend to the chickens at the farm.

Ken's father had a plot of land in Nova Scotia and Ken and Betty drove up there in September of 1948 to see the land and the rest of the province. It was a beautiful trip as the Fall leaves were plentiful and the countryside was peaceful and gorgeous. They camped on Ken's father's land for a night or two. The trip was the honeymoon they had never taken.

Carol

In May 1949, Carol Ely was born to Betty and Ken. When Betty had told him she was pregnant he said "Guess it will be okay if it is a girl!" Well, it was a girl, and she came into the world very small and quite jaundiced. She did outgrow that color eventually and seemed to be a happy baby. Since they were living with Helen and Hal, Helen soon became Nana. Betty gave up her teaching job to raise her child. Nana was very excited and happy to have a "granddaughter," and she fit her role of grandmother quite nicely. Carol was the third of the children born in 1949 to the Harding family: Carleen Reynolds was born to Laura and Leland Reynolds on January 13, and Gail Speirs was born in March to Donna Reynolds Speirs and Malcom Speirs. There would be four 1949 babies before the year was over, but, first, tragedy struck again.

CHAPTER NINE

Kate

In September of 1949, Kate Harding Reynolds died at home, surrounded by her family at the age of 63. She and her husband, D.G., had raised four children who were all married at the time of her death: Leland and Laura Gallup Reynolds, Doad and Chuck Jewett, Carol and Carroll (Beaky) Dunham, and Donna and Malcolm (Spike) Speirs. There were six grandchildren: Gary and Carleen Reynolds, Patricia and Lynn Jewett, and David and Gail Speirs. Carol was pregnant with her first child at the time.

The sisters all assembled with the immediate family for the funeral at the First Congregational Church of Lyme, along with Kate's nieces and nephews. The service was very nice, and the burial went smoothly. Kate's children placed single roses on the casket before leaving the cemetery.

Everyone then went to D.G.'s home on Route 156 directly at the junction with Sterling City Road. It was a large house and the group spread out within the downstairs kitchen, dining room and living room. D.G. was his stoic self; he never said a lot but he always listened. He was a businessman, running Reynolds Garage and Marina, with his son Leland. D.G. loved boating and he had a boat that he had named the DoCarDon in honor of his three daughters. The children loved the boating life as well, but Kate was not a fancier. So she would stay home while the rest of the family ventured off on week-end trips. She enjoyed the peace and quiet!

As the family milled around, visiting and eating from

all of the different dishes the sisters had brought, they were reminiscing about Kate.

Malcom made everyone smile when he told the story of asking for Donna's hand in marriage. "You know when I asked Kate's blessing to marry Donna she said she would pay me $5000 NOT to marry her!

Leland chimed in. "Mother was a character. Remember how she used to stay home when we would go boating with Dad? She said she enjoyed her peace and quiet!"

Carol spoke softly. "I just wish she had had an opportunity to meet our baby. She loved her grandchildren so much!

D.G. answered. "She was patiently awaiting that baby. She just didn't have the strength to wait long enough."

"Father, what will you do rattling around this big house all alone?" Leland asked.

"Well I'll tell you. I have asked Chuck to join the Reynolds team and manage the boatyard. He has agreed to do so and he and Doad will make their home here with me. It will be nice to have my granddaughters here.

Leland was stunned. "Well, that is a good thing, I guess. I didn't know Chuck knew how to run a boatyard and I am a bit surprised you went outside of the family."

Doad stared at Leland. "Chuck IS family, Leland, just as Laura is, and Beaky, and Malcolm. He has a business education and he is qualified for the job. I don't understand how you can question Dad's judgment.

Doad looked at him with disdain. Chuck left the room, presumably to refill his coffee cup in the kitchen.

"Uh huh. Well family is family and this business has been held within the family for more years than you or I have been alive. The men of the Reynolds family have made the business what it is today and they should be the ones to carry on the tradition." Leland replied. He then turned to Laura who was holding Carleen on her lap. "Guess we best be getting back down the hill to our place now." He looked over to where Gary and David were playing with a paper airplane. "Gary! Let's go!" And off the family went to walk back down the road to their home overlooking Hamburg Cove.

Doad watched them walk down the street. "I knew there was going to be a problem with Leland," she said to her father. "He thinks he is the only one who can do anything with the business. He will certainly expect Gary to join him when he is old enough to keep things in the family. But you can bet that if you had suggested that Carol, Donna or I take a role in the business, he would have really balked. According to him, only men have a business sense. That's why he will probably tolerate Chuck, or at least I hope he will. Can't say as it will be a good situation at any rate."

D.G. shook his head. "Doad, I wouldn't expect you girls to want to work in the business. It is a man's job. Leland is very involved in the garage and he feels responsible. It will be a long time before Gary is old enough to step in and help. I believed involving Chuck would make it as if you were more of a part of the business as well."

Doad looked at him. "Sure, Father." She said begrudgingly. She knew it would not be an easy path for Chuck either.

So Doad and Chuck moved into the house with Pat and Lynn, then 6 and 4 years old. There was plenty of room for all of them. Chuck made an office in one of the bedrooms.

Chuck spent most of his day at the boatyard, overseeing launchings, storage of boats, gas retail, refurbishing of boats, and other things that occurred daily. He was very conscientious and he was thankful to his father-in-law for his position. He found that Leland stayed mostly to himself overseeing the business at the garage and did not bother Chuck. Leland did have a boat, and when it was in the water it was docked in front of his home, not at the boatyard proper. Each month D.G. would have a meeting with the two men to discuss how things were going in both aspects of the business.

Doad was busy raising Pat and Lynn and she also did haircuts for her cousins' children. Carol was one of her regular customers and Betty would walk her to Doad's and have coffee while Doad cut Carol's hair and visited with Betty. Doad also spent a lot of time with her sisters, but her brother, Leland, kept mostly to his own family and the garage.

On Christmas Eve, however, there was always a Reynolds Christmas at Laura and Leland's. By 1950, it was a large gathering, with D.G., Carol and Beaky with Tip, Donna and Spike with Dave and Gail, Doad and Chuck with Pat and Lynn, and of course, Leland's children, Gary and Carleen. This was really the only time that the families all came together. Had Kate lived longer, there may have been more times for them to all enjoy each others' company.

CHAPTER TEN

Helen

In January of 1950, Helen Bull became the bride and wife of Allan Plimpton. It was a small wedding with Betty and Ken as witnesses. Helen did not want a church wedding because she was not overly religious and she didn't want to do anything that might involve the aunts. It was best to keep it simple.

Allan, better known as Bub, had returned several years earlier from a tour of duty in the Army in Europe. He was now working as a sheet metal worker at Speirs Plumbing in Old Lyme, a company owned by Allen Speirs, father of Malcolm.

Clarence had built the young couple a house on Bill Hill Road in Old Lyme, yet very close to the Lyme town border. Helen and Bub moved in to the house with their two cats, Lover Boy and Puff. Helen had grown very attached to Hazel and Clarence and her time with them had been a good fit for her. Now she had completed her business school, had gained experience working at the Selective Service Board, and was then working at the Old Lyme office of Champion Insurance and she loved her job and the people with whom she worked.

Every Sunday night Betty, Ken and Carol would come to the Bill Hill house to have grinders for dinner with Helen and Bub and watch TV. This tradition continued for years. The sisters and brothers also celebrated Thanksgiving and Christmas together, alternating which sister hosted which holiday. They were a close knit group. Carol loved being with her aunt and uncle any time they were together. Helen's birthday was the day before Carol's in May and they always shared a special cake with a chocolate nut frosting. Helen had a wonderful sense of humor that Carol thoroughly enjoyed.

Helen was a devoted Yankees fan and watched all of the games she could when she was not working. Bub had played on the Old Lyme High School baseball team, so he, also, enjoyed watching the Yankees.

Helen and Bub did not have children and were content to live their lives as they were. Carol took advantage of the fact and was quite willing to let them spoil her. Helen always held her grudge, however, against Ruth, Tess and Grace for the way they treated her after her mother had died. She spoke to them if necessary but did not go out of her way to see them. Betty, on the other hand, spent a great deal of time with them, visiting regularly with Carol. She knew how important family was and she was always offering to help her aunts in any way they needed. Betty wanted to instill in Carol family values and love for her family. By the time she was five years old, Carol had memorized the poem "Little Orphan Annie" and recited it willingly for each aunt whenever they asked for a performance!

Helen saw a lot of Hazel and when she was not working, the two would have coffee and visit. She also spent time with Mae, and with Nana when she was at Betty's. She was funny, and kind with these three aunts, and she avoided talking about the others, as if they did not even exist.

By this time Ruth had left the school in Essex and was teaching first and second grade at the Lyme Consolidated Elementary School. She hired Clarence to build her small yellow house just up the road from the Martin place, within easy walking distance of Helen and of the church. She became the church treasurer and was involved with the board that ran the church. Since Ruth lived alone, she came to have dinner with Nana every night but Sunday, when she fared for herself. She was not very domestic, so she arranged a deal to help pay for the groceries and Nana could do the cooking. Since they were close to each other, this arrangement worked out well for Ruth, and, as it happened, very well for Nana. Soon Ruth accepted the job of principal and first grade teacher in Lyme.

This was a very prestigious position and the sisters were quick to congratulate her. Ruth had worked hard throughout her life as she progressed through her schooling and did not seem to regret being the "old maid" of the family. It wasn't as if no man had been attracted to her. After all, Gib Miller, when a teenager, had thrown a black walnut at her and hit her square in the forehead. Ruth still had a scar from the incident. It was commonly known that boys would do such things to get attention from girls they liked. This ruse did not work with Ruth, however, and it was probably just as well since Gib became the town drunk in his later days.

Ruth spent a lot of time with Grace and Tess, especially. She was also the one who was closest to Elsie and to her grandson Clark. Betty and Carol were favorites to her as well. Without an immediate family, Ruth had the time to spend with her siblings and their children.

CHAPTER ELEVEN

Helen (Nana)

It was a Saturday morning and two year-old Carol was sitting on the floor of Nana's living room in the

Martin farmhouse, playing with her doll. Her mother worked at the Singer sewing machine creating a new dress for Carol, and Nana was baking ginger cookies in her kitchen. The aroma of the ginger cookies filled the house. Uncle Hal walked through the room, patted Carol on the head, and went on to the kitchen. He talked to Nana as he passed through,

"Going out to do some work in the shop, Helen."

"Okay," she responded, "See you in a while. Will you bring in some ground beef from the freezer when you come back?"

"Sure."

Uncle Hal went outside the house and walked slowly to the shop. The shop was full of old tools and wood, and a long workbench across the front window. The window looked out on Sterling City Road and to the pastures behind it. Betty continued her work on the old Singer sewing machine and Carol played happily on the floor.

Suddenly a loud gunshot rang out from the shop.

Nana cried out; "Oh my God! What has he shot?"

Betty chuckled. "Probably saw another woodchuck headed to the garden."

Nana looked out the window. "But he's not outside anywhere."

Betty stood up from the sewing machine. "I'll go check – keep an eye on Carol for a minute?"

Betty went out the door and headed for the shop. There was no sign of Uncle Hal outside so she entered the shop.

Betty screamed. "Oh no no no! Hal! Oh my God!"

Betty ran out the door and down the road toward her uncle D.G.' s house. She screamed "D.G. come quick! Something awful has happened to Hal! Help! Help us now!"

D.G. ran out of his yard and up the street after Betty. They went back to the shop and D.G. looked at his brother-in-law's body slumped on the floor, a bullet hole in his head.

Betty asked in a quivering voice, "Is he alive?"

D.G. answered, "I don't think so, Betty. We have to get the doc here. Go to Helen – does she know what has happened?"

Betty headed back to the house while D.G. went home to call the doc. Nana was at the door, visibly shaken

Nana was trembling. "What has happened? Why did you get D.G.?"

Betty touched Nana's shoulder. "Nana, Hal has shot himself. He is not breathing."

Nana was not accepting. "Oh no! He wouldn't do that! Why would he do that? He must be okay! It must be a mistake!" She ran out of the door, apron flying, to the shop and stopped as she looked in the door.

She screamed. "Hal!" She rushed in and cradled his head in her lap.

Nana cried. "Hal, wake up! You are all right! You are okay! Wake up! Talk to me!"

The tears began to streak down her cheeks as she realized that Hal was dead. Betty stood in the window of the house, tears rolling, looking out to the shop, holding Carol in her arms.

D.G. raced back in his truck with the doc right behind him. They entered the shop and D.G. gently brought Helen to her feet.

The doc examined Hal. "I'm afraid he is gone, Helen. I am so sorry. D.G., we need to get Mr. Jewett to come to pick up the body. Helen, let's get you back into the house. Betty will need to make some calls for you. You need to go and sit down."

Nana's apron and dress were covered with Hal's blood as were her hands. She allowed herself to be helped back to the house and sat down at the kitchen table. Betty came in and gave her a hug, helping her to take off her apron and wiped off her hands with a wet cloth. Nana could not speak. Carol watched from the door to the kitchen. Betty ran upstairs to get another dress for Nana and helped her out of the bloodied one.

Betty told Nana, "I am going to make you a cup of tea and then I will call the sisters. They will want to be here with you."

She put the tea kettle on as Nana sat at the table staring out the door. When the tea was poured it sat in front of Nana, untouched. Betty went to the telephone. She called each sister in turn and gave the same message.

"Something awful has happened. Hal shot himself in the shop and he is dead. Please come to see Nana and help her through this."

Each one responded with the statement that they would be there as soon as possible. The cars started to roll in the yard: first Ruth, then Tess and her husband Bill, then Hazel and husband Clarence, Grace and husband Al, Mae and husband Frank, and finally Elsie and husband Harry. The sisters clustered in the kitchen with Nana while the men sat in the living room, watching Carol on the floor with her doll. They were quiet.

D.G. and Betty were out at the shop with Mr. Jewett, the funeral home owner.

The men in the living room started to talk. Frank said, "I can't imagine what would make him do something like this. Something really bad must have happened. Is he ill?"

Al responded. "Not that I know of. He seemed to be doing his usual thing, taking care of the farm and the gardens. I sure didn't note anything unusual. What about you, Clarence?"

"No, nothing," Clarence answered. "He seemed okay to me. Hazel would have mentioned it if she thought there was a problem. You all know that!"

The men nodded.

Harry looked at the others. "I saw him last week. He seemed fine to me. We talked about the new cows he was going to get in the next month."

They all looked down at their shoes and sat in silence.

Meanwhile the sisters were in the kitchen. Grace, the youngest sister, was sitting next to Nana, the others were sitting or standing nearby.

Nana spoke with a shaky voice, "I, I just don't understand. I can't believe this. He didn't say anything except he was going to work in the shop. When we heard the gunshot, Betty said he was probably after a woodchuck and I thought so too. But I couldn't see him outside the shop!

"What have I done? What have I done?"

Grace took her hand. "You didn't do anything wrong, Helen. I have seen this happen in my nursing work; people get depressed and they don't see logical ways out of whatever hole they find themselves in. He must have had something really dragging him down. You know he never really talked about his feelings."

Hazel chimed in. "I bet it was the economy. Farming just doesn't provide enough income for all the hard work that farmers put in. I'll bet he was depressed about the economy!"

Ruth put up her hand. "Wait a minute – did anyone consider that maybe this was an accident? Maybe he was cleaning his shotgun and…"

Tess interrupted. "An accident? Really? From what D.G. said, the shot was right to the temple. That's no accident."

"Well, Ruth said, "we need to consider all angles."

Mae, the most quiet and naïve of the sisters said, "It is just so sad, Helen. What will you do?"

Grace answered for her. "What will she do? She will carry on as she always has. We will help you however you wish, Helen, and all you have to do is ask. We will plan the funeral with Betty. You can leave it up to us or you can be as involved as you want. I know this is a terrible shock for you. " Grace liked to be in control.

Elsie spoke to them all, "I think Helen knows we are all here for her. We are sisters and that is what sisters do when one is down."

Tess arose and poured tea for all the sisters, putting a fresh teabag in each cup. They continued to console Nana, each of them coming from a different angle. While they all cared for each other, they were also really ones who enjoyed being in each other's business, whether welcome or not.

The husbands waited patiently in Nana's living room. Of course no one thought to offer them tea. D.G. came in and joined them. "I think Helen has a whiskey bottle in the white cupboard there," he said. "I can certainly use a drink – anyone else?" All the brother-in-laws nodded. D.G. went to the cupboard and got out 6 small glasses and the whiskey bottle. He poured the brown liquid into each glass being sure they were all equal. When they all had their drinks, D.G. raised his. "A toast to Hal. Hope he is in a better place now." The others raised their glasses in silence.

Betty had taken Carol into her half of the house and she had called Ken who was at work. She told him what happened and he was on his way home. In the meantime her younger sister Helen came rushing in the front door.

"Oh my gosh, Betty, I can't believe this has happened. Did you find him?" Betty nodded, tears rolling down her cheeks. "What did you do?"

"I ran to get D.G. I thought we needed a man here and Ken was at work. I ran down to his house – I didn't even think about calling."

Helen looked at her. "This is just awful. Are all of he sisters here?"

"Yes. Along with Bill, Al, Frank, Harry and Clarence."

"Full house I guess."

"I guess. Grace seems to be in charge."

Helen frowned. "Ugh – she always is. Have they talked to you?"

"Not yet. I went in but they were all busy acting

consoling to Nana, so I just took Carol and came in here."

Helen smiled at Carol. "Well at least Carol is too young to understand."

Betty said, "We were in Nana's living room and the last thing he did before he went out was to pat Carol on the head. Oh God, this is so sad. Unbelievable."

Helen made her way past the uncles into Nana's kitchen where all her aunts were gathered. She noted that Tess, Ruth and Grace stiffened. She went over to Nana and gave her a hug.

"I am so sorry this has happened to you. Know that I will help you any way that I can."

Nana patted her cheek as the others looked on. Helen looked at the others.

Helen spoke to them. "Hello Aunties. So nice to see you but under terrible circumstances. I'll be next door with Betty if anyone needs me."

She turned away smirking. Grace, Ruth and Tess shook their heads. It was evident that there was no love lost between them and young Helen.

The day of the funeral was cloudy but mild. Services were held at the church with a burial in the church cemetery. Nana spoke at the gravesite. "I just want to thank everyone for their support and for being here today to honor Hal's life. Family is so important, as are friends, but family relationships are the key to support and appreciation of all."

The family and some of Nana's friends gathered at the house. Carol was toddling around looking at all of the people dressed in black, drinking tea or coffee and speaking in hushed tones. She was showing them her doll and the pretty dress her mother had made for the doll. She heard bits and pieces of conversation.

Hazel was in a corner talking with Ruth and Tess. "Can you believe some people are saying that Helen was running around?"

Carol looked at Hazel. When she heard "running around" she knew that Nana ran around after the chickens. She went to find Nana and lay her head on Nana's lap. She understood Nana was sad.

Ruth responded, "That is just ridiculous. Where did you hear that?"

Hazel said, "People talking at the funeral. They mentioned having the boarders at the house and all. Of course there is only one now and Pete is very young."

Tess was outraged. "Hazel! You aren't suggesting…"

Hazel backed up. "I am not suggesting anything. I'm just saying what I heard."

Ruth said, "Well I think it was depression. I think that probably things weren't going as well economically as Hal wished. He probably felt he couldn't take care of Helen."

Tess replied, "Well that's an odd way to solve the issue. What a horrible thing to do to Helen."

Grace, overhearing some of the conversation came over to the small group. "People don't think about the effects suicide will have on others. They are too preoccupied with their own problems and they don't see their way out. We need to support Helen."

Carol wandered among the guests, carrying her doll. The aunts smiled at her, patted her on the head, and asked about her doll. Carol knew each one but there were so many there all at once that she had trouble keeping them straight.

The men were collected in the front room with plates of food, talking in hushed voices. The women were gathered in Nana's living room. Betty was in her kitchen with young Helen, putting out the food and drink.

Finally the few friends who joined them said good-bye to Helen and made their way to their cars. The family remained and spread throughout the house. Hazel and Mae went into Betty's kitchen to talk with her.

Hazel asked, "What will you do now, Betty? I mean with the farm animals and all?"

She looked at Hazel. "Well for now we will carry on. I can do the work that Hal did as far as milking and feeding. Nana will need to decide if she wants to sell them. We certainly will keep the chickens. I just don't even want to think about it right now."

Mae jumped in. "Of course you don't, dear. Just helping Helen through this should be what you are concerned about. Grace says we should be sure that we visit several times a week and call her every day we don't come over."

Young Helen responded sarcastically. "Well, Grace would surely know what should happen!"

Hazel approached Helen. "Helen, Grace has a nursing background and she knows about these things. Let's keep personal feelings out of listening to her now."

Helen came back. "Yeah she is really kind and caring. Right."

Hazel put her hand on Helen's shoulder. "Look this is one situation and yours is another. The rift between you and Ruth, Tess and Grace is another thing all together. You don't have to interact with them if you don't want to, but you could at least be tolerable when you are with them."

Helen retorted. "Why should I be the one who is tolerable? They don't even speak to me. Betty is the favored one. And, you know, that doesn't even bother me. She does so much for all of you…let her be the favored one. You all probably don't even appreciate all that she does."

Mae spoke up. "Helen! You know we love you. You were not only Maria's child but you were also ours after she died. I never had children and you are my child as far as I am concerned."

Helen thanked Mae and gave her a hug. "I know you care, and so do you, Hazel. The others just make me so angry! They are so pompous. At least I don't have to interact with them other than these situations. Thank God these are not frequent encounters."

Betty turned to her sister. "I know you have a right to be upset with Ruth, Tess and Grace; but right now our focus has to be on what Nana needs and she loves you too. With a family as large as this one, we are bound to have some family squabbles."

Helen answered Betty. "This is not a squabble; it is pure nasty treatment. Oh well, I don't really care."

No one noticed that Ruth had been listening at the doorway to the kitchen. She shook her head and walked back to the sisters. Carol still wandered from group to group. She found Nana and crawled up on her lap. Nana hugged her close. Nana was the only "grandmother" Carol had.

By the time that the family members left Nana's house for home, Nana and Betty were both exhausted. Nana headed upstairs to her bedroom where she doused herself in her favorite *Save the Baby* liniment and donned her nightgown. Carol loved the scent and associated it with Nana and bedtime. As Carol crawled into bed, Nana came in to her room and rubbed her back while Betty read her a fairy tale. Carol drifted off to sleep.

CHAPTER TWELVE

Time passed on and soon Carol was four. It was August and it was traditional that the Hamburg Fair was held on the third Saturday every August. Since Nana's home was almost adjacent to the fairgrounds, the side yard became a place for the sisters to come and sit to enjoy the sounds coming from the fair: the oxen and horse pulls, the calliope music, and the square dance music at night. They wandered down Sterling City Road to the fairgrounds and spent time actually at the fair, visiting with friends and neighbors as they watched the events. People came from all over the county to the quaint little fair.

There were always flying swings, and sometimes a ferris wheel as well. The upper fairground had games that could be played to win beautiful ceramic statues or stuffed animals. At the end of the games was a tent housing chickens and rabbits entered on display. A pony ride was located on the hill as well. Large horses and oxen also waited on the hill for their turns to compete in the drawings of cement blocks, determining the strongest teams in the county.

Frosty orange sodas, popsicles and cotton candy were favorite treats. The Grange Hall had flower arrangement competition and bakery contests on the first floor, and upstairs there was a schoolkids' exhibition of artwork as well as handicraft displays. Nana always entered braided rugs and table runners as did Hazel.

There were hotdogs and hamburgers, ice cream, lime rickeys, and many other goodies to consume. There were many colored balloons and toys on sticks.

This year that Carol was four was perhaps her most memorable year for the fair: she took her first pony ride. Nana held her by the hand as they climbed the hill to the pen where the ponies were. Carol's hand was sweaty because she clutched Nana's hand very hard, but Carol was determined. The man at the gate with the green cowboy hat asked her to wait for the next pony to come around the ring. As the pony approached, he seemed very big to Carol. Her heart began to beat rapidly. A little boy with tear-stained cheeks was lifted off, his tears having dissolved into a smile. The man with the green cowboy hat tried to lift Carol onto the pony but she said "I can do it myself."

She gripped the pommel of the saddle and started to

put her foot into the stirrup, but the cowboy laughed. "You are on the wrong side, darlin'! Come over to this side." Carol switched to the other side and placed her foot in the stirrup as she gripped the pommel. She swung her leg over just like she had seen Annie Oakley do on TV on Saturday mornings. The pony felt so good and warm, and he smelled of hay, oats and all other good things ponies like to eat. She leaned forward and hugged the pony around the neck; he felt so good and cuddly. And then the cowboy led them around the ring while Carol held the reins and grinned from ear to ear. She waved to Nana who smiled and waved back. Then at the end of the ride, Carol dismounted and handed a lump of sugar to the pony. He nibbled it gently from her hand and then went on around the ring with another little girl on his back.

Carol waved good-bye to her pony and skipped back to Nana. "That was so much fun, Nana! Do you think Santa Claus will bring me a pony for Christmas if I ask and if I am a very good girl?"

"Well, he just might," Nana said, taking Carol's hand and heading to the wooden bleachers where a few of the sisters were sitting.

"Hi Ruth! Hi Tess! Hi Grace! Did you see me on my pony?" Carol bubbled with excitement. "Nana said maybe Santa Claus will bring me a pony if I am a very good girl! Wouldn't that be great?"

Ruth looked at Nana. "Helen, you better watch what you say in front of the C-H-I-L-D. Betty and Ken might have something to say about all of that." Carol was busy asking Grace if she had a quarter that Carol could have to ride on the high swings.

"Let the child dream, Ruth. Who knows, we have the barn. Maybe Santa WILL bring a pony!" She laughed. She called to Carol. "Let's go home and get some lunch, Carol. Your Mom is making cucumber sandwiches today. Then we can come back later."

"Can I ride on the high swings when we come back? Grace gave me a quarter!"

"Put it in your pocket where it will be safe and we will come back to the rides after you have your lunch. Did you thank Grace?"

"Thank you Grace!" Carol called. "I'll come back later and ride the swings. You could ride them with me!" Grace waved.

Nana and Carol made their way out of the fairgrounds and back up Sterling City Road to the house. The group in the side yard had grown and Carol could see her mother and father, Mae and Frank, Elsie and Harry, and her cousin Clark. "Clark is here, Nana!" she said with excitement. "He can ride the swings with me. Can he have a cucumber sandwich with me too?" Without waiting for an answer she ran to Clark and the two scrambled up the branch of the maple tree in the side yard. They giggled together while Betty went inside to get the cucumber sandwiches.

Nana sat down to visit with the others in the lawn chairs. "Ruth, Tess and Grace are all down at the fair waiting for the oxen pull," she said. "I haven't seen Hazel yet but I did see that her bread won first prize in the baking contest!"

Mae smiled, "She always was good at baking and cooking in general. I'm happy for her that she won first prize. I think that will earn her a dollar!" Elsie smiled too.

Betty came out with the sandwiches and called Carol and Clark. They jumped from the branch and ran over to her. "Clark says I was brave to ride the pony, Mom! He wants to do it too. Can we take Clark to the pony ride Mom? Please?"

"Sure we can. But first have your lunch and a bit of a rest. Then I will take both of you back to the fair."

The children gobbled down their sandwiches with excitement. In the meantime, Hazel and Clarence arrived. Hazel was as anxious as the children to get to the fair. Clarence was happy to sit and talk with Harry and Frank. "Go ahead down, Hazel," he said. "We will be along when we hear them getting ready for the oxen pull."

Hazel looked at Mae, then Elsie, then Betty. "Okay," Betty said, "The kids are anxious to go so we will head down there with you." No one told Hazel about her blue ribbon for bread – they wanted her to see it as a surprise. The four of them headed off, Carol and Clark running ahead.

Carol led Betty to where the aunts were sitting. Hazel had gone in to see the exhibits at the Grange Hall. She would be pleased when she saw her blue ribbon. "Okay it's time for the swings!" Carol was excited. The aunts said they would watch from their seats because they didn't want to lose their good view of the ring where the oxen pull would be. "Will you wave at me?" Carol asked. They assured her they would. It would be hard to dismiss a four-year-old's enthusiasm.

Carol and Clark each paid the man their quarters and he helped them up into their swing seats. He carefully hooked the chain in front of each of them. When the ride started, Carol started waving in the direction of the aunts. It was so fun, whirling around high above the ground. Carol and Clark both swung their legs back and forth as they rode. When the ride came to an end they waited patiently for the man to come and get them from their seats. They ran to Betty, very excited. "Can we do it again Mom, huh?" Carol begged.

"Later you can have another ride. Right now we are

going to get you some cotton candy and we will all settle down to watch the oxen pull."

"Yay! Cotton Candy!" the two children yelled in unison.

The men had come down, along with Elsie, and were there with the sisters. Hazel had come from the grange and was beaming. "What's up Hazel?" Clarence asked.

"Well! I won first prize for my bread! That means I win a dollar AND I can enter the county fair!" Hazel was delighted and the sisters smiled as Grace just shook her head.

"Good for you, Hazel!" Clarence said. And they all settled down to watch the oxen competition.

The afternoon passed along and the children were getting edgy. "Time for Clark's pony ride, Mom!" Carol pulled at her arm. "Can I ride again too?"

"How many quarters do you have?" Betty asked. Carol reached in her pockets and came out empty-handed.

"Maybe Daddy has quarters," she said quietly.

"I have exactly two quarters," Ken said, and Harry handed Clark two quarters. Off the children skipped toward the pony ride with Betty following closely behind.

That night Carol lay in bed, listening to the sounds from the fair, the music from the square dancing and the announcements from the ring for the horse pull. She smiled and closed her eyes. "Only one year to wait for the next fair," she thought, "and maybe Santa Claus will bring me a pony." Suddenly she opened her eyes – "I forgot my prayer!" she said to herself. She looked at the sampler that Nana had made that hung over her bed. She couldn't read yet but she knew it by heart: "Now I lay me down to sleep, I pray thee Lord my soul to keep. If I should die before I wake, I pray thee lord my soul to take. If I should live for other days, I pray thee Lord to guide my ways. Amen. God Bless Mommy and Daddy, Nana and Blackie, and everybody on earth and everyone in heaven, And, God, please send me a pony for Christmas!"

CHAPTER THIRTEEN

Tess

In May of 1954, just after Carol turned five years old, the telephone rang and Betty answered. "I will be right there – have you called the sisters? Okay I will have

Nana do that." She hung up and ran in to where Nana was working on her sewing machine.

"Tess just called and Bill has not come back from his morning chores at the farm. She can't find him anywhere in the barn. Can you call the sisters and tell them? I am going to go help look for Bill."

Nana nodded and shivered as she recalled the incident where Hal had disappeared into the tool shed and then killed himself. She went to the phone and started the calls. Betty took Carol and headed to the Early Dawn Farm.

"Where are we going?" Carol asked.

"Tess is looking for Bill and can't find him so we are going to help," Betty answered, a sense of dread in the pit of her stomach.

When they arrived, Elsie was just pulling in with Althea, her daughter and Clark's mother. Clark was with them and he had a wrapped package. "Here Carol! This is for your birthday!" Carol was excited and opened the package to find a make-it-yourself jewelry kit.

"Carol," Betty said, "You and Clark stay here and play on the porch. Tess is inside if you need anything but try not to bother her. I will be back as soon as I can." She crossed the road with Elsie and Althea. One by one the sisters were pulling into the yard. Soon many were on a search party for Bill in the fields. Carol and Clark played happily on the porch with the jewelry kit.

After about an hour of searching, Betty was the one who found Bill lying in the back pasture where the bull was standing over him and had apparently gored him. It was a muddy and bloody scene. Bill's body was bruised and his clothes were torn. Once Betty was able to get the word out that he was found, the men carried the body back to the house; the bull following obediently to the barn. The doctor determined that Bill had suffered a cardiac arrest and conjectured that the goring was because the bull was trying to pick him up. It was a gentle bull that never would have hurt Bill to begin with. Bill was 67 years old.

They laid Bill's body on a sheet over the couch in the parlor to await the coroner and then the funeral director. Tess bustled around the kitchen, not seeming to know which way to head, or what to do.

Tess was heating hot water for tea to give to the searchers, and as they piled in the house they were an overwhelming group. As she always did, being the frugal sister, she put out exactly two teabags for all to share (usually it was just one, but this was a big group). Luckily some said they were going to head home – they were emotionally and physically exhausted. Therefore she did have enough cups for those who stayed. As they sat and sipped the somewhat weak tea (one dip of a bag in each cup was the policy), Tess thanked everyone for their help. "I just don't know what I will do without Bill. I can't run the farm by myself," she stated. She was visibly shaken, as would be expected, but she was able to converse and she was glad to have the company. Ruth said she would stay there with her overnight.

Grace suggested that Tess go and lie down for a while. "What for?" Tess asked. "There are chores to be done. I have to milk the cows, I have to pick the beans, I have to…" and her voice trailed off as she sank into a chair.

"Tess," Grace said, "We can all help you by doing the chores today and we can figure out how everything will get done after that. You have a great deal to think about, and first of all we must arrange for a funeral for Bill. Mr. Jewett will be here to discuss that with you. Do you want me to call the minister?"

"No," Tess said affirmatively. Bill was not religious. "We will do a graveyard service."

"So you would want the minister for that," Ruth interjected.

"No," I think we will just be at the grave when they put Bill into the ground. He was a quiet man, he wouldn't want a fuss."

"Well, " Grace said, "Let's see what Mr. Jewett proposes.

When Mr. Jewett arrived with the hearse to take the body, Tess gasped as he was taken out of the house. "Why did this happen to me?" she cried.

Mr. Jewett came back in to discuss the details. "You already have a plot at the church cemetery, Tess. I assume that is where you want Bill to go."

"Yes. But I don't want any fuss. Bill wouldn't want any either."

"Well, it would be best to have family there when he is interred. You can choose a casket that you think he would like and we will have the body prepared and placed inside. We can do this as early as tomorrow if you are not planning a public service. I assume you want an obituary in the newspaper."

"How expensive is all of this?" Tess asked.

"We can use a plain pine box if you wish; the obituary cost depends on the number of words."

"Make it short, then. Just enough so that people know he has died."

"All right, and we will say that burial is at the convenience of the family."

"We can do this tomorrow?"

"Yes, I will have the grave dug in the morning and let's say we can proceed about 3 P.M. at the cemetery. Will that work?"

"Yes. The sooner the better."

Grace and Ruth just looked at Tess and accepted her thoughts. After all, she was the widow, even though she may not be thinking clearly.

Ruth said, "I will call the family and tell them about the 3 P.M. gathering. What do you want to do afterwards?"

Tess asked "About what?"

Ruth responded. "Well usually the family gets together over food and drink to reminisce."

"Bill wouldn't care about that," Tess insisted.

"But Tess, your family cares about you and will want to be with you. Let's see if we can have the gathering at the Martin house."

In the meantime, Helen had been wandering aimlessly around her home waiting for word of what had happened. When Betty and Carol came home, Betty told her how they had found Bill. "I must go to Tess," Helen said. "She needs support. I know how it is."

"Do you want Ken to take you?" Betty asked.

"No, I will drive myself" and off she went.

Later that day Betty took Carol and went over to Hazel's house for coffee and to talk. "That Tess," Hazel said, "Can you believe that she uses one teabag for so many cups? And then she saves it in case they want another cup!" My mother nodded and sipped her coffee. Carol sat and sipped some milk. Hazel continued, "She probably has more money than all of us with that farm, and she is so cheap! Clarence went to the bathroom today and what did he find instead of toilet paper? Rags! Can you believe that? She washes those rags and re-uses them!" Hazel would never say anything to Tess, but she enjoyed talking about her.

Betty said, "Well, there will be some changes in her life now. She will have to make some decisions, especially about the farm animals. I doubt that she will hire anyone to run the farm."

"And spend a penny?" Hazel scoffed. "Surely not. I think she will sell the animals. She can do the garden herself."

"Maybe she will re-marry," Betty said.

"I doubt it," Hazel retorted. "Who would want to live with her?"

The report in the newspaper read as follows: "May 16, 1954 – William C. Peck, 67, owner of Early Dawn Farm on Lord Hill, was killed by a bull yesterday in a pasture about a half a mile from his home. His body, as described by State Police as 'badly bruised,' was discovered by his niece, Mrs. Kenneth Plimpton, about seven hours after he had gone out to repair the fence. State Police said Mr. Peck had been tossed about 'quite a few times,' and most of his clothing had been torn from his body. State Police Sgt. D. W. Mielke said mud on the head and hooves of the bull was the same type as found on Mr. Peck's body. Mr. Peck's family became concerned when he failed to return from his work and a searching party was organized. His body was found by Mrs. Plimpton about 5 P.M. Mr. Peck was born in Lyme May 15, 1887, the son of Richard and Jenny Davidson Peck, and he had always lived at the Peck homestead. He served as town selectman for several years and had held offices in Crystal Lodge of Odd Fellows. He was married to the former Theresa Harding, a teacher, on July 25, 1928. Funeral arrangements are pending."

Since the newspaper did such a good job, Tess did not feel she needed to bear the cost of an obituary.

The funeral as planned was a small one with just the family attending. Bill had been a quiet farmer after his terms as selectman, and did not involve himself much in the community of Lyme. Tess had purchased a plot in the cemetery behind the church; Hazel allowed that it must have been relatively cheap for Tess to do that when there was still room in the Harding plot. Bill was laid to rest amidst little fanfare and the family gathered at the Martin house for refreshments. Nieces Doad, Carol, Donna and Betty made the tea and had furnished a supply of homemade cookies. Therefore, the tea was strong and good; even Tess acknowledged the good taste.

In 1956, Tess married D.G. Reynolds, her brother-in-law. D.G. moved to the Early Dawn Farm from the center of Hamburg and parked his Mercedes in the garage. The farm was no longer functioning as Tess had sold off the stock. D.G. was busy at Reynolds' Marina, building his own boat, the High Dawn. This boat would later be christened by his granddaughter, Carleen, and launched in 1959. Tess, like her sister Kate, was not into boating and was glad to have the grandchildren accompany D.G. on his sailing exploits.

The two of them lived together until 1976 when D.G. died. They seemed to be an amiable couple, both with good senses of humor, and, despite the weak tea, the family enjoyed going to visit with them. D.G. allowed that his wife was a bit "tight on the purse strings," so his spending was cut significantly. He did make sure there was plenty of wood for the fireplace in winter as Tess was very frugal with the heating system at the farmhouse.

CHAPTER FOURTEEN

The First Congregational Church of Lyme stood on the northwest end of Sterling City Road, facing Hamburg Road (Rte. 156). The church was white with blue shutters and had a steeple that housed a huge bell that generations of children liked to sneak in and ring on Halloween night. The church had been there for many many years, actually built in 1814, and it was vibrant and healthy in membership during Carol's youth. In earlier years the Harding children were delivered by their father in horse and wagon to attend the service, and their father, Lyman, would head down the hill and visit with his son-in-law, D.G., and then pick them up again after church.

Carol's mother and father were married in this church. They did not, however, attend as regular members of the congregation.

When Carol was five years old, Betty and Ken started sending her to church with Nana. Several of the Harding girls were regular attendees at the

Church and were also members of the LBS, Ladies' Benevolent Society. Nana, Ruth and Hazel all sat in the same pew. Carol would sit in the front pew with her cousin, Carleen Reynolds, also five years old. Carleen's mother, Laura, was the choir director and she sat in the front pew next to Carleen and led the choir in its usual presentation each Sunday. The little girls were always dressed up, complete with Mary Jane shoes. Halfway through the service the children would head downstairs for Sunday School.

Carol never gave much thought to the fact that her mother and father didn't go to church. She went happily with Nana and she loved Sunday School. On Children's Day in June, she sang "Jesus Loves Me" with a group of preschoolers to the congregation.

The Church held an annual Christmas pageant and the sisters would all come when Carol and Carleen were in the cast. In Carol's first pageant she was "the angel with the runny nose" as she asked for a Kleenex right in the middle of the performance. "How cute," the sisters agreed.

When Christmas came, Carol was still hoping that Santa would bring that pony. Grace and Al took Carol and Carleen to a big department store in Hartford, CT. They always laughed when they told the story of how Carol told Santa, "You can bring me anything you want, and I'll be happy!" It seemed she was too star-struck to remember the pony request!

Time passed and when Carol was ten she was old enough to join the junior choir at the church. Carleen's mother, Laura was the director and any girl who wanted to join could do so. Therefore, Carol was never daunted by Laura's admonitions to "sing softer, Carol!" Being in the choir meant wearing a maroon robe and white collar, marching into the church in order of height to front seats during the opening hymn. Carol often told others with pride, "I am the shortest so I get to go first!"

The very best part about being in the choir was at Christmas times when they would all get in one of the Tiffany Farms' hay trucks and travel through Lyme to different parishioners' homes, singing carols. It was so much fun. They would stop and exit the truck at a couple of places for hot chocolate. A few of the sisters were on the route for the caroling. Nana was first, then Ruth and then Hazel. Those sisters who did not live on Sterling City Road, or were not church goers, did not see the carolers. Carol liked to be with her best friend from next door, Nancy Adams. Nancy was really cool. She was an alto in the choir and hardly moved her lips when she sang. She was not only Carol's best friend, but also her idol.

Nancy and Carol often felt that Church at 11 AM each

Sunday was an inconvenience. "It really messes up a good play day," Nancy would say, and Carol would readily agree. And when the service changed to 10 AM in the summers it was even worse! But their parents insisted that they go, and go they did.

Nancy and Carol liked to play in the cemetery behind the church. Many of the stones made excellent "horses" to ride, and there was a dump over the wall where old flower arrangements were tossed. They liked to scavenge in the dump to get pieces of styrofoam or plastic flowers and small toys. One day Clark was visiting and they were exploring in the cemetery and Nancy noticed that there was a stone askew atop of a grave that sat a bit above ground level. The children peeked in but they couldn't see anything.

"Let's get a flashlight," Nancy said. "Go ask you mother for one."

Carol, always eager to please Nancy, went back to her house and interrupted the Garden Club meeting that Betty was hosting.

"Mom?" she said.

"What is it, Carol?"

"May I have a flashlight?"

"What for?"

"Nancy and I found a hole in a grave and we want to look in it to see what is there." She answered.

The Garden Club ladies giggled politely while Betty blushed and told Carol that was inappropriate and that no, she could not take a flashlight to the cemetery.

Carol left the house with her head hung low.

The three children decided to "ride" the monuments like horses. Clark read the name on his. "Lyman Darius Harding age 24. How do you think he died?"

Nancy and Carol shrugged their shoulders.

"Can you die from getting hit?" Clark asked.

Nancy answered. "It probably depends on how hard you are hit and where."

"I don't want to die," Clark said.

Carol looked at him. "You are young. You won't die now."

"But Grandma Elsie hits me."

"But Elsie is nice to me!" Carol said. Clark shook his head.

"Not nice to me and my Mom."

Nancy said "You should hit her back."

"I couldn't," Clark said.

"Why not?"

"It's not right to hit people."

Nancy was frustrated. "But she is hitting you. If you don't want to die, you need to do something."

"I don't want to play here anymore today," Clark said. As he walked back to the Martin house, the girls joined him.

*****

One day when Carol was in fifth grade, she was playing at Carleen's house. They were in a room that had a picture window overlooking Hamburg Cove, and the TV and games closet were in that room. Laura came in and said, "Girls, come here for a moment and sit down. I have something to tell you." They did as they were asked and looked expectantly at Laura.

"I just received a telephone call with some sad news that I think you should know," she said. "Dr. Ross died yesterday while he was on his trip to Venice." Dr. Ross was the only minister I had ever known. His wife, Blanche Ross, was our Sunday School teacher.

"What happened?" Carleen asked, wide-eyed.

"Apparently he had a heart attack on the ship."

"Is he in Heaven now?" Carleen asked.

"Probably so," her mother answered.

Carol did not say a word. This was the first death that had occurred in her life, of which she was cognizant. When Hal took his own life she had been too young to understand or even remember. She had not truly grasped the concept of death when Bill Peck died when she was five. She was curious about Mrs. Ross and how she would act when she came back. Carol then said, "I think I feel like going home now."

When she got back to her house, Carol saw her mother in the kitchen. "Did you hear about Dr. Ross?" she asked her mother.

"Yes, dear. Ruth called with the news and Nana has been on the phone ever since. It is very sad, don't you think?"

Carol did think it was sad and the death affected her deeply. She had dreams after that of seeing him wandering through Nana's bedroom and walking through the halls in her house. She always awoke frightened by the dreams. When Mrs. Ross came back, she handled the situation with grace and continued their education in Sunday School without missing a beat. Each Sunday there was a substitute minister until the church finally found Dr. Euston who took the job permanently. To this day, lights illuminate the front of the First Congregational Church in memory of Dr. Ross.

CHAPTER FIFTEEN

Carol in First Grade

In September of the year that Carol was six, she started her schooling in the first grade. When she was five she had become aware that her cousin Carleen had learned to read! Carol went home to ask her mother to teach her too. Her mother said, no, that she would learn soon enough in school. It was at that point that Carol took her Little Golden Books that she knew so well and taught herself to read! Therefore she entered the first grade with her newly acquired skill.

She felt excited about school because her teacher was her great aunt, Ruth. Ruth was a first and second grade teacher as well as, by that time, principal of the Lyme Consolidated School. She had been the most educated of the Harding children, having graduated from business school and then Willimantic Normal School. Being the only sister never to marry, she seemed content with her lot in life and she enjoyed the children and her work at the school.

Carol and Carleen were both in the first grade and easily adjusted to calling Ruth "Miss Harding" during school hours. They took pride in the fact that they could read already and were in the "high" reading group, where there were also second grade students. Each classroom at Lyme Consolidated had two grades, and the assignment to classroom seemed to be related to each child's aptitude. Therefore the second graders who were in Miss Harding's class were the slower students in the second grade. As Carleen and Carol progressed through the years they were always in the "higher" half of the class.

Each morning the children in Miss Harding's class would sing a song together and then say the Pledge of Allegiance, with hands held over their hearts. Reading groups were next and each one had a special time with Miss Harding at the front of the room while the other children worked on spelling and vocabulary words. Arithmetic was a full class subject, as was science and social studies. Recess was twice a day and there was a direct route to the outside playground from Miss Harding's classroom. On some days there was art or music with Mrs. Thomas or Miss Miller. For art, Mrs. Thomas would come into the classroom and for music the children carried their chairs to the auditorium where Miss Miller sat at the piano. Lunch was in the basement cafeteria and children could bring lunch from home or buy a hot lunch. Carol had a Roy Rogers lunchbox.

Carol loved going to school because there were so many children to play with. She especially liked Kevin Mazer, better known as K.C. She referred to him as her boyfriend and Carleen claimed Graham Beckel (Buddy) as hers. They liked to play at recess and the merry-go-round was a favorite. It had long chains from the top that had handles on them that the children would grasp, run and swing out as the pole turned. It was great fun. They also played on the swings and challenged each other to go higher as well as to jump off while the swing was in flight. Carol was never one to back away from a dare! Amazingly they never were injured while on the playground!

Yes, school was fun, even in the classroom. When it was time for Art sometimes they we able to do cutting and pasting. Mrs. Thomas would give each child a glob of white paste on a paper to use when putting together pictured on construction paper. The best thing about the paste, Carol thought, was the taste! She loved to lick her fingers off after pasting something together. It was the best!

Both Carol and Carleen excelled in their schoolwork and they passed easily into second grade for the next year. Mrs. Davis was their teacher.

She was a really nice lady and the children in the class loved her.

At one point during the year, Mrs. Davis suffered an appendicitis attack and was out of school for what seemed like several weeks. Betty helped Carol call all the children in the class to ask them to bring 25 cents to school to help pay for a gift for Mrs. Davis. Carol felt very grown up doing so, and it was her choice to buy the pretty tissue box cover from Mrs. Emerson, mother of Jamie Emerson in her class. Betty was the substitute teacher while Mrs. Davis was out. Carol couldn't call her Mrs. Plimpton, so she didn't call her anything.

When Mrs. Davis came back she thanked the children for the gift and for their drawings and notes that had been sent to her. She assured them that she had missed them all. Carol had to tell her that she was the one who orchestrated the collection of money and the gift. Mrs. Davis gave her a hug.

Third grade came along and Mrs. Cushman was the teacher. Clara Cushman was a large, older woman with white hair. Third grade was where cursive writing was introduced and Carol loved making rows and rows of O's as practice. The thing that the third and fourth graders in Mrs. Cushman's class remembered forever was that Mrs. Cushman died in the Spring. Carol was the first student who knew it as her mother was the substitute and Ruth had called early that morning. When the school bus arrived at the school, Buddy Beckel was jumping up and down yelling "Old Fatty died. Old Fatty died!" Well, she was, indeed, dead and Betty was to take over for the remainder of the year. Carol found herself spending a lot of time in the hallway for doing this or that that her mother found inappropriate. Looking back on the situation, it was probably because Betty wanted to be sure to show no favoritism to her own daughter. Earlier in the year Ruth had told Carol "The only reason that you get all A's on your report cards is that the teachers want to please me." Carol was smart and she was sure she deserved what she earned. It was never really clear to her why Ruth said that to her, as Ruth was never mean to her in other instances.

Fourth grade brought Mr. Bennett to Lyme Consolidated. His claim to fame was that his mother dated Brad Davis, the Dick Clark of WTIC TV Hartford. Brad Davis hosted a dance party show for teenagers. Mr. Bennett was very strict. One day Carol's reading group was working with him and they had their workbooks open and were going over answers. Mr. Bennett caught Carol erasing and changing some of her answers to the right ones after the group had gone over the answers. He was angry with her and she tried to tell him she was just being sure the right answers were there. In fact she was cheating so she would get an A on her workbook. She was glad he did not tell Ruth what she did.

Fifth grade had a new teacher, Miss Eileen Burke. The children loved her, with the possible exception of Russell Rand. Russell was one of the sixth graders and he lived in Sterling City. One day he was angry with Carol for something she had done, and he showed her his middle finger under the desk. Carol ran immediately to tattle to Miss Burke, who came over to Russell and slapped him across the face! The children sat in stunned silence; of course they did not know what Russell had done.

Russell hung his head at his desk.

Later when the children were at recess, Carol said sarcastically to Russell, "See what happens when you do something dirty?"

He looked at her in anger. "She said that if you say anything about it you will get the same treatment." Carol walked away, not wanting to be slapped for saying something she shouldn't.

This was also the year that Betty was substituting in Carol's class and was reading to the children after lunch. Carol decided to use her pencil and fully color the surface of the formica desktop. When her mother saw it, she sent for the principal – Ruth! When Miss Harding came in and saw what Carol had done, she sent Carleen to watch her own classroom while she watched Carol wash the desk. Carol didn't think it was a big deal as you could just spit on it and the pencil would come off! At any rate, Carol rode the bus home that day to avoid riding with her mother and Ruth.

At the end of the year somehow the children learned that Miss Burke was being fired. They, of course, could not understand, but they were not given reasons. A "committee" of students went to Miss Harding to beg for Miss Burke to keep her job, but it was to no avail. Carol never did learn what had happened to cause Ruth to dismiss Miss Burke.

At the end of Carol's fifth grade year, Ruth retired

from the Lyme school. A reception was held at the school on Sunday, June 19, from 4 to 6 P.M. in her honor. To celebrate her 12 years as principal, members of the community and former pupils and residents were invited to attend. Ruth had been involved in teaching for 34 years. Over 250 guests paid tribute to Ruth where a "gay and colorful" reception was held. Ruth was presented with a white crystal watch from the community at large, as well as a pewter cream and sugar service with engraving on the tray "From the Children of the Lyme School." She was attired in a navy blue dress with a white orchid corsage for the reception.

When sixth grade arrived, Carol and Carleen found themselves in Mr. Tedesco's classroom. He was a fun teacher and his students enjoyed being in his class. He also had a part-time job selling men's clothing at a store in Essex, CT. Carol's friend, Betsy, was over to play one Saturday and they were riding their bikes and decided to go to the school. They found that the door to the first grade classroom was unlocked and they sneaked inside. In the first grade room they erased the board that held the words to the morning song and wrote "Hi First Graders!" in big letters. Then they went to the sixth grade room and opened the files and looked through report cards. They knew they were doing something that they should not do.

On Monday morning, they were summoned to Mr.

Perrucio's office. He was the new principal. They sat in chairs in front of his desk. He looked at them over the desk and began to speak. "Apparently someone broke into the school this week-end and wrote some things on the blackboard in the first grade room. Our custodian, Mr. Langworthy, said he saw the two of you playing on the playground on Saturday. I am wondering if you saw anyone hanging around the school while you were here."

Shaking in their chairs, they both shook their heads, indicating that they had not seen anyone just hanging around.

"Well," Mr. Perrucio said, "Think about it and if you remember anything come back and talk to me about it."

The two girls slunk out of the office. Little did they know that he was quite sure that they had been the ones to enter the school.

When they were alone, Carol said "What are we going to do?"

Betsy shook her head. "I guess we better tell the truth. But let's not tell him about the report cards."

Carol nodded. "Let's go back and tell him." But Mr. Perrucio had left the building for a meeting so the girls went back to their classrooms to stew about the problem. Mr. Tedesco asked Carol what was happening and she told him. He agreed that telling the truth would be the best thing to do.

They had to wait almost all day before Mr. Perrrucio returned. They met with him and soberly confessed to entering the school and writing on the blackboard. "The teacher had a lot of work to do to re-write the morning song on the board," he said. "Now, I am going to have to call your parents. You will stay inside for recess for two weeks and you will be assigned times to help the teacher in the first grade classroom during those recess times. I will tell your parents what your punishment is." The girls just looked at him, wide-eyed.

Carol asked quietly, "Do you have to tell our parents?"

"Yes, I do." He replied.

When Carol went home that day she knew she would be in for punishment at home as well. Since her mother was a teacher, she ALWAYS sided with the teachers if Carol were in any sort of trouble, which had happened from time to time. When she came in the kitchen door, Betty was ready. "Have a seat, young lady."

Carol did as she was told. "Tell me what you did at the school on Saturday," Betty said.

"We went in the first grade classroom and erased

the board. Then we wrote 'Hi First Graders!' on the board."

"And why did you do that?"

Carol shrugged. "It seemed like fun at the time."

"Well, when your father gets home we will discuss your punishment. I am sure you can expect to be grounded for quite a while."

The rest of sixth grade went by peacefully enough, and in the Spring Carol and her friend Priscilla Sturges went to Williams Memorial Institute in New London to take an examination to enter the private school in the Fall for seventh grade. Betty believed that Carol needed more direction and discipline and that WMI was a good school, grades ranging 7-12 and all girls. She planned to go back to teaching, this time first grade in Old Lyme, so they could afford to send Carol to private school.

Carol's mother dropped them off for the test and Mrs. Sturges picked them up afterwards. She asked what had been on the test and she was told that one part was to write an essay on any topic desired. She said, "Well, what did you each write about?"

Priscilla spoke first. "I wrote about how to make a rock collection."

"Really?" said Mrs. Sturges. "I guess that is appropriate since you have one. Carol, what did you write about?"

"My first pony ride at the Hamburg Fair."

"Now, that is a wonderful topic. You chose well, Carol!" Carol smiled.

They were both accepted into WMI for the Fall of 1961. Ruth questioned Betty on the need to send Carol to a private day school, as she felt the education in Lyme was good enough. Betty explained the discipline angle and the advantage of small classes. Ruth agreed that Carol did have a tendency to get herself into trouble; not that it was serious trouble but that it was bothersome. "She seeks attention in the wrong way!" Betty said.

Hazel congratulated Carol on her acceptance to WMI. She had sent her son, Bob, to the Buckley School in New London and believed that private school was the best thing to do. The other sisters didn't have much to say about it. After all, it was Betty's decision to make and if she was willing to work to make it happen then that was all the better.

Carol loved going to WMI for all of the six years. In her Freshman year, a new headmistress, Miss Marion Hamilton, came and changed the school's name to The Williams School. Carol really liked Miss Hamilton and she found ways to get into trouble that was serious enough to be sent to the Headmistress, but not serious enough to impair her educational opportunities. Carol really liked her physical education teacher who arrived in Carol's sophomore year, Miss Rosemary McGuire. To get attention from her, Carol left an anonymous note in her office saying "I hope you manage to let everyone know who your pets are." It was kind of ironic as Carol really was one of the "pets." As Carol was heading to study hall, she passed by Miss McGuire's office. Miss McGuire said, "Carol, I need to talk with you."

Carol liked that feeling that she got in the pit of her stomach when she sensed that she was in trouble. She followed Miss McGuire into an empty classroom and they sat down. "I received your note," Miss McGuire said.

Carol nodded. She did not deny that she had written it. "I find it disturbing that you think that way, and also that you did not sign your note."

Carol said "Sorry."

"Well," Miss McGuire said, "I showed the note to Miss Hamilton and she wants to talk to you."

Carol could feel the excitement in her stomach of trouble brewing for her. She nodded again.

"So," she is waiting to talk to you now."

They walked to Miss Hamilton's office and Miss McGuire went in first. Then she came out and sent Carol in. "Sit down please," Miss Hamilton said. Carol did.

"Miss McGuire came in yesterday and said 'I have received an anonymous note,' and I said 'From Carol Plimpton, I would guess.' So to be fair, we went through all of the schedule cards that students fill out at the beginning of the year to see which ones matched the penmanship on your note. Yours matched perfectly."

Carol nodded and placed her hand over her stomach.

"Carol, it is a very serious issue to send an anonymous note. And it is inappropriate for you to accuse Miss McGuire of having 'pets.' Just who do you think you are?"

Carol knew she had gone too far this time. She shrugged her shoulders and looked down at her shoes.

"Look at me," Miss Hamilton said. Carol did. "You have been in my office far too many times for me to overlook. I know you are seeking attention but you are doing it in the wrong way. I do not believe that this is the right school for you."

Carol gasped. She loved the school and the teachers. She had lots of friends. "May I have a second chance?" she asked in the smallest of voices.

Miss Hamilton looked at her and waited to respond. Carol's stomach had turned from excitement to sickness. "Of course you may ask for a second chance. And I believe in second chances. This is what I want you to do. I want you to write an essay about this experience and what you have learned from it and I want that on my desk Monday morning. Secondly, I want you to tell your parents what you have done. I am not going to call them, you are going to tell them. Have I made myself clear?"

"Yes, Miss Hamilton, thank you," Carol said quietly.

"Did you apologize to Miss McGuire?"

"Um, no, not really. I didn't say very much to her about it. I mostly listened."

"Then you will use the rest of your study hall time sitting in the foyer and writing a note of apology that you will sign!"

"Okay."

"Do you have anything else to say"

"I am sorry for my actions, Miss Hamilton. This will never happen again."

"I am certain that it will not. Now go write your note

to Miss McGuire and I will see you when you arrive Monday morning."

Carol took the meeting to heart, and as difficult as it was, she did tell her mother what she had done. Betty was furious and she called Miss Hamilton that afternoon. She told Miss Hamilton that she was mortified by Carol's behavior and that punishment would occur at home. She thanked Miss Hamilton for giving Carol a second chance. Carol was then grounded for two weeks; Betty never told Ken as she thought he would say they should stop wasting their money on private school and put her in Old Lyme High School. Betty did not want that.

Carol was on her best behavior for several months. It could not last forever, but her transgressions in her last two years did not reach the serious level of that one time. Miss McGuire continued to be her role model and when Carol chose a college, she chose Russell Sage College in Troy, New York, because it had a physical education teacher education program. She wanted to be a teacher like Miss McGuire.

Carol received an early decision admission to Russell Sage and was notified at the beginning of her senior year at Williams. This was very exciting opportunity and Carol took full advantage of the early decision to relax and let her schoolwork take a back seat. After all, she was already accepted so why should she work hard for good grades now? Mediocre would do!

When Spring came of her senior year, Carol was still content with C grades, and was enjoying her year. One day, never being one to turn down a dare since she and Nancy jumped off the chicken coop, she decided to be the first girl in history to cut a class at the Williams School. She chose senior English and she hid in the library for that class period. The next class involved a math class so she went to study for a test. Then school was over for the day.

When Carol arrived home, the telephone rang.

"Carol?" Miss Hamilton said.

"Yes."

"Were you in senior English class today?" she asked.

"No."

"Why not?"

"I was studying for a math test."

"Thank you. Good-bye," Miss Hamilton said quite firmly.

Carol sat down with a sigh. Okay, she had been busted!

Now what? It was a Friday and she had a job babysitting for the Tiffany's. While she was there she called Mrs. Whitlock, her English teacher, to apologize but Mrs. Whitlock would not talk to her. She stewed about what to do. The next morning she told her mother what she had done. Of course her mother was angry and, again, mortified that her daughter would behave like this. On Monday she called Miss Hamilton.

"Mrs. Plimpton, we are tired of Carol's shenanigans. This is what we have decided. I am not going to say a word to Carol about this. But I will tell you that if she gives Mrs. Whitlock, or any other teacher, any trouble, she will fail that class and will not graduate from Williams. In addition, she may not participate in any extra-curricular activities after school."

Betty said she understood and she apologized for her daughter's behavior. "I can assure you that Carol will put her best foot forward for the remainder of her time at Williams. Thank you for your concern and for sharing this information with me."

Carol was grounded for a month and her driver's license was taken by her mother for that time as well. She would be riding the bus.

It was a good thing that Betty shared the information with her daughter, and Carol set an example of good behavior from that time on. She again apologized to Mrs. Whitlock. After graduation she said to Miss Hamilton, "I thank you for all you did for me. I bet I am the first one you were ever happy to see go!"

Miss Hamilton smiled and shook her head. "You were a challenge, my dear. But I am not happy to see you go. I AM happy to see you move on to college to prove yourself. Let me know how it goes."

Carol was thrilled with the invitation to stay in touch.

College was wonderful and Carol loved every bit of the traditions of Russell Sage. She did well enough in her classes and she made life-lasting friendships. In her junior year she was a "Big Sister" to a girl who sought her attention constantly. It was then that she wrote to Miss Hamilton. It was an "I get it now" letter where she expressed that she had figured out that she had been such a pest because she wanted the attention. She could see the pattern of behavior that her "Little Sister" was displaying and she realized that was her own pattern at The Williams School. She received a beautiful reply from Miss Hamilton, thanking her for writing, and acknowledging her learning. Carol was to see Miss Hamilton again several times, and the last time Miss Hamilton was in her 80's and joined a few girls from Carol's class for lunch at the Griswold Inn in Essex. Mrs. Whitlock brought Miss Hamilton to the gathering. Miss Hamilton acknowledged that there was always something special about that class of '67! And Carol still thought Miss Hamilton was pretty special!

Carol graduated from Russell Sage in May of 1971. Her education continued at The Pennsylvania State University (Penn State) for a year and then she began teaching physical education in Lake Placid, New York. She taught and coached for 10 years, then going to The Ohio State University on 1982 to pursue her doctorate in Motor Development, Physical Education. Then in 1985 her education was completed and she accepted a position as Assistant Professor in Teacher Education Physical Education at The University of Toledo, Toledo, Ohio. Hazel and Grace were the only aunts living at the time to see her success, and Grace really could have cared less.

CHAPTER SIXTEEN

Hazel

Hazel and Clarence had married in Spring of 1921 when Hazel was 22, and their son Bob arrived four years later, in 1925. Bob had a somewhat difficult childhood because expectations were very high for him.

Bob

After he decided to run away from home in his younger years, he went to the Mill Pond to hide. When Hazel found him, she took him home and tied him with a clothesline when he was playing outside. As he grew, he expressed his frustrations with his mother by throwing the chicken's eggs at the garage door. That did not endear him to his parents at all! His parents sent him to the Buckley School in New London instead of to Old Lyme, where he wanted to go. When he turned eighteen, Bob enlisted in the army. As he was leaving, his father shook his hand and said good-bye.

At it turned out, Bob was a war hero, and in August 1945 he was awarded the bronze star medal for heroic achievement in connection with military operations against the enemy in northern Luzon. The citation read: "When an attack on enemy positions in mountainous terrain was halted by intense hostile fire, a mortar squad of which Pvt. Lee was a member, was called forward to assist in the attack. He helped set up the gun under the concentrated Japanese fire, and commenced firing. Although an enemy shell burst in the immediate area and stunned him, Pvt. Lee continued his mission and assisted in knocking out two Japanese positions and killing fifteen enemy soldiers." Hazel and Clarence were very proud of their son.

After his service, Bob attended the University of Michigan where he earned his degree in Architecture.

Carol remembered Hazel as the aunt who dropped in frequently for coffee, usually en route to or from church, after an LBS (Ladies' Benevolent Society) meeting, garden club, shopping, etc. And she remembered going to Hazel's where her mother would have coffee and she could have milk or tea. Hazel could be seen driving everywhere, usually down the center of the road (after all no one else was using that space at the time) and hunched over the steering wheel similar to a tortoise humping a rock that it thought was another tortoise! She was a very cautious driver, stopping at every intersection whether or not a stop sign was present. It was probably a good thing that Clarence did the driving on longer ventures.

Over coffee, she and Betty would hash over the events of the day, week, or month that usually involved other members of the family. This was where Carol learned a great deal about the idiosyncracies of her great aunts. Nana would often come in and join the coffee time but she was pretty quiet about her sisters. Being critical did not appear to be one of her traits.

Hazel was a wonderful cook and baked the best bread ever! She maintained a vegetable garden in the summer and a grape arbor as well. She raised chickens in a pen at the back of the garage. Hazel was also very handy in making braided rugs and table runners. Probably her claim to fame, however, was her use of the telephone. She did not hesitate to call to complain if a workman had not done something right, if a package arrived with the wrong contents, if her new nylons ran immediately upon donning, if the date on a recently purchased item was a day over its limit, or if she needed to tell the doctor about a predetermined ailment. And, if she called once, she called 4-5 times. In the meantime she would call Bob daily, if not several times a day. It was very significant that at her funeral the telephone at the funeral home rang during the service.

In 1952, Bob married Mary Jane McWhorter, of Burgettstown, Pennsylvania. He had met her while he was in school in Michigan where she worked as a nurse. Hazel and Clarence, Grace and Al, and Betty went in Clarence's car for the drive to Western Pennsylvania for the wedding. Hazel appeared to be the radiant mother of the groom, but later showed her true colors in her jealousy of Mary Jane. Bob and Mary Jane made their home in New York City where Bob was working in an architectural firm.

When Carol was four, Betty dressed her in a brown velvet skirt and jacket, complete with tam, and they went with Hazel on the train to New York City to visit Mary Jane and Bob. Mary Jane tried her best to please Hazel and took them to see "The King and I" on Broadway. Carol grew bored and so Mary Jane took her out to see the toys at FAO Schwartz. Betty and Hazel were able to enjoy the show. When they went back to the apartment, Carol was playing on a swing outside and another child wanted the swing so he slapped her. Carol was not happy about that and ran crying to her mother. That was the end of the playground time. The next day they took the train home. Carol liked the train ride.

Bob and Mary Jane eventually moved to West Hartford, CT, where Bob and a partner established the firm of Lee and Crabtree. In December of 1953 their son, Robert Harding Lee II (Bobby) was born. Hazel was in seventh heaven. She and Clarence made many day trips to West Hartford and they would usually take Carol along to see her cousin. Carol absolutely loved Mary Jane and treasured the time she had with her.

In October 1955, Hazel's second grandchild arrived, Virginia Lee (Ginny). Nothing could make Hazel happier than being with the grandchildren. When Bobby and Ginny were older, they would come to visit and stay for a few days in Lyme with Hazel and Clarence. Hazel loved driving them to each sister's house to show them off. She and Clarence continued to take their Sunday visits to West Hartford as well. And Carol began to spend time there, staying for a week at a time and absolutely loving it.

Bob designed a home for his family in Simsbury, a suburb of Hartford, and it was a very modern, open design. In 1961 Susan Lee joined the family, followed in 1963 by Catherine Lee. The family was complete. By this time, Carol was going to school at WMI and had different vacation times than her mother had in Old Lyme. Therefore she spent her vacations with the Lee's in Simsbury and grew closer to her cousins. Hazel was again excited about the births of the two youngest children and loved to visit. Bobby, however, was always her favorite.

Mary Jane was a wonderful mother to her children and spent a great deal of time with them doing projects, going to special places, etc. Hazel was highly critical of her housekeeping skills. She talked about her behind her back, complaining that her son was used to a tidy place and now he had to live in one that was not so well kept. It was probably true that she was suffering from her jealous streak, that Bob preferred Mary Jane to her, and that Mary Jane had the children, everything that Hazel would have wanted. Bob was impatient with her constant telephone calls and questions, and Hazel was sure that Mary Jane was putting him up to his impatient ways with her.

In the meantime, Hazel resented the fact that when Bob and Mary Jane were in town they wanted to spend time with Grace and Al. Grace had formed an attachment to Ginny, feeling that Hazel's favoritism for Bobby overshadowed Ginny, and Grace decided she would shower her attention on Ginny. Hazel hated the fact that Grace was able to have so much time to visit with them when they were there such a short time, as was usually the way. The other sisters loved seeing the Lee's and their children but they did not demonstrate any preferential treatment toward one or the other.

When Bobby and Ginny were in high school, Bob took a job in New Jersey, and moved the family to Devon, PA. Hazel had a conniption fit. She could not understand his moving so far away. The drive was at least four hours, and she would not have the Sunday visits that she lived for. The phone calls continued and most probably increased in frequency after the move. Hazel was convinced that Mary Jane put him up to this move. She told Betty more than once that Mary Jane told Bob what to do all the time.

Hazel had to adjust to Bob's career move, and she settled back into her life at "The Place" as she called their home. She had to be contented with visits as they occurred and she and Clarence went a few times to Devon.

Quite a few years later, on one visit to Hazel's, Betty found Hazel ironing and crying. "What is wrong?" Betty asked.

"Poor Clare – poor poor Clare," Hazel said between sobs.

Clarence shuffled through the kitchen. "Ridiculous!" he muttered.

"What is going on?" Betty asked.

Hazel took a big sniff and blew her nose. "They called from the hospital and we have to get Clare there right away! He's going to die! I know he is going to die! What will I do without him? What will happen to ME?"

Clarence shuffled back through the kitchen and looked at Hazel and then Betty. "Ridiculous." He repeated.

The phone rang. It was the hospital. They had called the wrong Clarence Lee.

Hazel went through a period of manic calling on the telephone to everyone she knew and was in a general panic about Clarence's health. She was basically driving numerous people crazy so Betty called Bob and said it was time for a visit. Bob and Mary Jane came right up.

They went in to assess the situation and saw that Hazel was totally exhausted. They decided to go ahead with the contingency plan they had worked out. "Mom, let's go over to Betty's for coffee," Bob said. "Get your jacket and we will go in our car."

While Hazel and Mary Jane made their way to the car, Bob talked to his father. "Dad, Mom needs a rest. We are going to take her with us back to Devon. Can you take care of yourself for a week or so?"

"I guess." Clarence replied evenly.

"Okay, call us or Betty if you need something."

Hazel sat in the front and Mary Jane in the back. She asked why they were going out by Tiffany Farms to go to Betty's. "Well, Mom, we aren't going to Betty's. We are taking you home with us for a while."

"What? You are NOT!" she exclaimed.

"Yes we are. You have been driving people crazy up here and you need a rest from all of this confusion."

"But Clare…"

"He knows and he will be fine. It's just for a little bit."

"You have no right to take me with you!"

"Well, we are, and you will just have to accept it. We will welcome you to our home."

"Does Betty know about this?"

"Not yet."

She turned to Mary Jane in the back. This is your fault – you told him to do this to upset me. You have always hated me."

"That's not true, Grammie," Mary Jane said. "And we are going to take care of you for a while. You need rest."

Hazel folded her arms across her chest and refused to speak to either of them, eventually falling asleep.

When they reached Devon, they took her inside and upstairs to a bedroom. Mary Jane gave her a nightgown, towels, a toothbrush and toothpaste. "Do you need help getting ready for bed?" she asked Hazel.

Hazel just stared at her so Mary Jane went to her own room to go to bed.

The next day, Mary Jane took her shopping for clothes and out to lunch. They came home and Hazel fell asleep on the couch. At dinnertime the granddaughters came to see their grandmother. Bobby was living and working out of state. Hazel was still not happy that she was there and she was not pleasant to anyone. Mary Jane took her to see gardens, to do more shopping, to fancy lunches, and Hazel would sleep in the afternoon and again all night. Finally she said she wanted to be back in Lyme in time to vote in the election. Bob and Mary Jane thought that would be all right.

They took her home the Monday before the election. She had been gone one week. She had talked to Clarence on the telephone and he had assured her he was fine. Once Bob and Mary Jane left, she picked up the phone and started her calls. She told both Grace and Betty how she had been kidnapped and abused. Mary Jane was very mean to her, she said, and she would never trust them again to do what they said. It was Mary Jane's fault, not Bob's, as he would never do anything like that without being told to do it.

Then she went upstairs and unpacked the new dresses and other clothes that Mary Jane had bought for her.

One day, after Clarence had died, Hazel was going to Christmas dinner at his relatives' home. On Christmas Eve she called and Carol, then a teacher living in Lake Placid, New York, and home for the holiday, answered. "I am not going to dinner tomorrow," she said.

"Why? What is wrong, Hazel?"

"I can't find my garters anywhere. I can't go without my garters," she answered.

"Do you want me to come look for them?" Carol asked.

"Yes." So over to her house Carol went.

They retraced her steps and even looked in the trashcan. Well, Carol did find the garters. The Harding girls had an idea that flushing the toilet once a day was enough, regardless of what was in the bowl. When Carol looked in the toilet, there were the garters.

"I found them!" she called to Hazel.

She came in and looked in the pot and said "Well

look at them floating in all that shit!" She reached in, grabbed them, and rinsed them in the bathroom sink. She then put them on a radiator to dry. Luckily she could then go to Christmas dinner the next day.

Hazel was truly a character. One of her favorite things to do was to visit Dr. Von Glahn. Her primary concern was that she had what she called a "carbuncle" in her nether regions and she liked to have him check the growth. Carol often felt empathy for poor Dr. Von Glahn, who actually pre-deceased Hazel. Perhaps it was an escape tactic!

CHAPTER SEVENTEEN

Ruth

It was a pleasant day when Ruth decided she would take Tess "across the river" on a shopping trip. They always felt that prices were better in Old Saybrook than in Old Lyme, so they would make the trip every couple of weeks. Tess, being the frugal one, was always happy to have the opportunity to go as she had given up driving when she married Bill Peck. By this stage in her life she had lost Bill, and had remarried to her brother-in-law, D.G. As Ruth and Tess rode along, they rehashed the week's events and caught up on the traditional gossip. In order to get to Old Saybrook, they had to cross the Connecticut River on the Baldwin Bridge, which was also I-95, the Connecticut Turnpike where the speed limit was 60 mph. Ever cautious, Ruth chugged along at a good rate of 25 mph. Tess was talking non-stop about this or that and staring straight ahead. She asked Ruth why she was slowing down and Ruth didn't answer. Tess thought that was rude so she looked over to the driver's side and noted Ruth was no longer there! She had fallen out of the red Studebaker Lark while she was leaning on the driver's door as she always did. It wasn't as if the weather caused any issues so Tess thought she should turn off the engine. When she looked back, sure enough, there was Ruth on the pavement of I-95. The story was never quite clear about what happened next, other than Leland's garage was called and he brought a wrecker to get the red Lark. Ruth had some bumps and bruises and was taken by ambulance to the Shoreline Clinic, but was otherwise okay and was picked up by Betty and taken home. Tess allowed that she had always told Ruth she shouldn't lean on the driver's door as she drove. The red Lark was repaired, took up residence in Ruth's garage, and it never crossed the river again. That was undoubtedly a good choice.

As an independent woman, Ruth enjoyed living on her own in her retirement, in the little yellow house on Sterling City Road. She often took Nana and Carol with her the opposite way from the river on I-95 to Niantic to visit her sister Elsie and her husband Harry. Of course Ruth drove, leaning on the driver's door, and off we would go with Carol in the back seat and Nana up front. This meant that Carol would be able to visit and play with her cousin Clark who lived across the street with his mother and father, Althea and Russell. These visits happened throughout Carol's childhood.

On one occasion, when they were driving home, Ruth said to Nana, "Did you see those bruises on Clark?"

Nana winced. "I did. You don't think Althea did that, do you?'

Ruth looked straight ahead. "Maybe."

Nana answered. "I don't know. We have all seen Elsie's mean streak. You must remember when she beat Althea after finding out she was pregnant… Can you believe beating your daughter because she thought the pregnancy would take attention away from her?"

Ruth replied. "I don't think Clark is a problem. I wonder why she would beat him."

Nana answered. "Maybe there is more to the story. Clark is your favorite."

CHAPTER EIGHTEEN

Elsie

Clark had been born in November of 1948. Elsie was
a very devoted mother to her daughters, Althea and

Lucille. When Althea became pregnant with Clark, Elsie perceived that attention would go to the baby and Elsie would be left out of Althea's life. When Althea first told her about the baby, Elsie was incensed.

"Whatever would possess you to have a baby?" Elsie said in anger. "You have a good job at the bank. Having a baby is going to ruin your life."

"Mother," Althea answered, "I thought you would be happy to have a grandchild! Russell and I are thrilled. What a blessing this is!"

"A blessing?" Elsie sneered. "You call this a blessing? Honestly Althea you are just a whore!"

"Mother!" Althea exclaimed, "I am a married woman who wants a family. How can you call me a whore? That is just mean."

"You are a whore, that's what you are. You just couldn't stay out of bed or this wouldn't have happened. I can't believe you are actually happy about this."

Althea started to cry. "You had two children. Were you a whore?"

"Harry wanted children. I never did."

"So you didn't want us? I thought you loved us!"

"I do, I suppose. But I certainly did not expect you to get yourself pregnant."

"How is it different from what you did?" Althea said tearfully.

"I can't even stand to look at you now. Get out of my sight," and Elsie smacked Althea across the face. "Go home to your precious husband and be happy with him about this. You have betrayed me!"

Althea ran out of Elsie's house and across the street to her house. Russell was shoveling snow off the driveway. He saw Althea running toward him and he took her in his arms and into the house.

"She's nothing but a bitch," Althea said. She should be happy about a baby, a grandchild."

"Althea," Russell said quietly, "Your mother has always insisted on controlling your life. This is something she can't control and she is probably going to be jealous of this child. He or she will take your time away from her and she can't face that."

"So I am supposed to just accept her attitude and go on as if nothing is wrong?"

"No," he said. "Give her time to cool off and then just go along with your life as usual. Do not take any guff from her. If you are with her and she turns mean, leave. Don't even bother to fight back. It is not worth it."

"Maybe we should just move away."

"Now you are getting to be a bit extreme." Russell said. "When this baby comes she will turn around and love him or her just as we will."

"You are dreaming, Russell."

"Probably I am."

Althea's relationship with her mother remained tense for the next 8 months. When Clark was born, Elsie and Harry came to the hospital. "Where is this wonder child?" Elsie asked Althea.

"He is in the nursery. He is wonderful, Mother. You are now a grandmother! Go see him, you will love him."

Elsie turned on her heel and strode out of the room. "Come Harry," she directed.

When she looked through the window into the nursery she saw him right away, Baby Boy Creswell. He looked like the typical big-headed newborn baby to her. "What's the big deal? " She thought. "Just some distraction that Althea will use to avoid spending time with me. I hate this."

"Harry, let's go see Lucille. At least she isn't silly enough to get herself pregnant."

"She isn't married," Harry said quietly.

"Well, if you recall, that didn't stop Grace."

Lucille did marry a few years later, to Courtland Clark. She became Lucille Clark Clark! Elsie did not seem to be threatened by the marriage; in fact, she was glad that Lucille had found a husband. In the meantime, Elsie became somewhat accepting of Althea's baby, Clark, but she resented the time that Althea spent with him. As he grew older, he spent time with Elsie and Harry and sometimes they even kept him overnight. To keep him supervised, they pushed their twin beds together so he could sleep between them.

Elsie was not what one would call a "warm" grandmother. She expected Clark to behave, and when he did not, as boys could be, he would receive a slap or a spanking immediately. Surprisingly, this did not deter him from pushing the limits. "Incorrigible, " Elsie said.

It was Clark's daring spirit that Carol liked best. They would climb trees, wrestle, and even slide down sand piles in cardboard boxes. Carol knew that Clark always let her win when they wrestled. She never saw Elsie's mean side as it did not show when Ruth and Nana were visiting with her.

When Clark was 18, he had been living a life of challenging behavior. Elsie was beside herself. It was unfortunate that she died before seeing him marry, raise two wonderful girls, and turn his life around. In the 18th year of Clark's life, Elsie died. Her husband, daughters, their husbands, and Clark were all at her side.

When Nana received the telephone call regarding Elsie's death, she again expressed the fact that "It should have been me. I am the eldest."

CHAPTER NINETEEN

In the Spring of 1968, Robert Kennedy was campaigning to run for President of the United States, and Carol was finishing her freshman year at Russell Sage College, in Troy, New York. As a physical education major student she had a requirement to attend two sports camps and her first was to be with the Red Cross at Water Safety Instructor School on Lake Hayward near Colchester, CT. This would be for a week. Her aunt Helen was going to take her there as her mother was still teaching.

On Sunday morning at about 5:30 AM the telephone rang. Since there was an extension in Carol's room she answered. It was her uncle Bub. "Put your father on the line," he said, abruptly.

"Dad," she called to the room next door. "Phone for you."

"Who is it?"

"Don't know."

Ken went downstairs to take the call. "Hello?" Then there was silence as he listened. Then Carol and Betty both heard him say "We'll be right there, Bub."

He came back upstairs and into his room. "What is it?" Betty asked.

"Helen passed away in her sleep." Carol heard him and gasped.

"Oh my God!" Betty exclaimed. She got out of bed and dressed quickly and then she came into Carol's room. "I will call you when I know what is happening. In the meantime I think you should go to work (Carol worked at the local Hallmark Ice Cream Shop in Old Lyme in the summers) just as you had planned." Then she ran down the stairs and out the door after Ken.

Carol lay in her bed, not knowing what to say or think. All she could think of was her uncle Bub and the song "I Will Leave You Softly."

Since she did not have to be at work until 11 A.M., she dressed and went downstairs to await the call. After about an hour her mother called and said that Uncle Julian had been there and said that Helen had died. It was probably a blood clot since she had just been dismissed from the hospital after a D&C procedure on Friday.

Helen had had heart problems in the past few years and they had tested her heart while she was at the hospital and the doctor had told her that all was well and that if she continued her medication she would live a long life. Carol was stunned – after such good news, to have this happen, was just terrible.

Betty came home after a while and Ken stayed with Bub. Just after she entered the house she heard Nana's phone ringing the double ring for Ruth who was on the party line. Of course Nana picked it up anyway. "Oh no," Betty cried out, "I wanted to tell her and be with her when she heard." She knew the call was from Hazel, informing the sisters of Helen's death. Betty raced into Nana's parlor to be with her as she heard the news.

Nana sat at the phone, receiver in hand. She looked at Betty and said, "It should have been me. I am the eldest and it should have been me." Helen was 42 years old.

As it turned out, Betty sent Carol to the camp on her own in their Volkswagon, with a letter requesting permission for Carol to come home to attend her aunt's funeral on Wednesday of that week. Carol was still in shock.

On Wednesday, many family members gathered in the Centerbrook Cemetery in Ivoryton for a graveside service for Helen. She was buried with her mother and father. A blanket of red roses lay on the grave. Bub stood with Betty, Ken and Carol. Hazel, Clarence, Mae, Frank and Nana were there. Afterwards they gathered at Mae and Frank's. Visibly missing were Ruth, Tess and Grace.

Hazel was inconsolable. "I just can't believe this. She was so young. It can't be true; it just can't be true."

Mae patted her on the shoulder. "Sometimes we just can't explain things that happen. It is a terrible thing but at least she didn't suffer. You know she had been through a lot of health issues in the past couple of years."

Betty looked at them and said "Remember Mother was not very old when she died, just 50 years old. And it was determined that it was her heart."

Bub sat quietly on the sofa, listening to Helen's family. "At least THEY didn't have the nerve to come to the service," he said in a tone just above a whisper.

Hazel replied. "No, and I am glad they didn't come. Helen would not have wanted any of them there. They all said they were sorry to hear that she had died, but I didn't expect them to be here to pay their respects. Grace even suggested that maybe Helen would now be at peace. Can you imagine saying that?"

"That family is never at peace," Bub said. "There always

has to be something underlying their behaviors. The way they treated Helen should never be forgiven. At least I will never have to deal with them again."

In fact, Ruth, Tess and Grace had gathered at Grace's house for lunch that day. Ruth sighed, "I suppose we were right not to go to the service."

Grace looked at her in astonishment. "Of course we were! Helen was nothing but problems for us since Maria died, and she carried her grudge through into her adult life. She didn't care about us, whereas Betty does. The two sisters were very different."

Ruth sighed again. "Grace, WE held a grudge against her as well. It was a mutual agreement that was never made in person. I do feel bad that she died, and at 42 no less. She had so many more years left! I don't think Maria would have wanted us to be so hard on Helen."

Grace retorted. "We had to be hard on Helen because she was misbehaving and trying everyone's patience. Betty didn't do that. Nana never had a problem with Betty. Helen was rude and inconsiderate. I told Hazel that maybe she could now be at peace."

"I am not sure I will be at peace," Tess said. "I am thinking that maybe we were wrong about Helen and just didn't handle the situation the right way."

Grace spoke tersely. "Helen was a difficult child who

became a difficult adult. It is unfortunate that she died so young but I am not going on a guilt trip over what we chose to do. There are always two sides to each story and our sisters are blinded to the facts."

They ate their lunch in relative silence as no one really felt up to reviewing the latest town gossip. That would be what they would usually do, or discuss the other sisters.

In the meantime, the gathering at Mae and Frank's came to an end, and Bub left with Betty, Ken and Carol. Hazel and Clarence were on their own. Bub had agreed to be at Betty's for dinner on Monday nights and Hazel's on Thursday nights, at least for a while. He knew he was welcome at other times as well.

That evening Betty and Ken took Carol back to the aquatic camp at Lake Hayward.

CHAPTER TWENTY

As Nana aged, she became a bit difficult to care for, and Betty hired a part-time caretaker to help her with doctor appointments, shopping, and companionship. Nana's doctor had told her a drink a day wouldn't hurt her; Betty became aware of how much alcohol had been purchased and where it was hidden! Perhaps she should have let her drink as it improved her temperament! One night when Carol was home from college, Betty served swordfish for dinner. Carol loved to soak her fish in lemon and so she went to Nana's kitchen to borrow the bottle of lemon. She poured it all over her fish but it didn't look right and tasted worse. Whiskey! It was Whiskey! And there went another hiding place down the drain.

Betty tried her best to keep up with all of the remaining aunts, Nana, Mae, Tess, Ruth, Hazel and Grace. She was especially busy with Hazel, helping her pay her bills and organizing her life. She visited them all and was on call for anything they might need. She was still teaching in Old Lyme so she was balancing family and work as well. Nana was then 85 and was not able to get around easily. She used to grow frustrated when Betty asked her to do something she didn't think was necessary, and she would say "I hope you get old like I am and see what it is like!"

Still Betty persevered. On a particularly stressful day she told Carol, "When I am old, take me kicking and screaming to a nursing home, do NOT feel you have to take care of me at home!" Fortunately that never did have to happen.

When Carol was in her senior year at Russell Sage College, she received a telephone call from Betty, "Carol, Nana died this morning." She had been in failing health for several months and she slipped away in her sleep. This was the second close family death in Carol's life and she didn't know what to do, other than to pack and head for home. She loved Nana very much; she had been the grandmother that Carol never would have had.

On the 3 hour drive home, Carol's head filled with memories. She recalled the night, when she was four, sitting with Nana watching "The Lawrence Welk Show," and sucking her thumb.

"Tsk. Tsk! Carol! Why are you doing that again?"

Carol continued to suck her thumb and nestled closer to Nana.

"Do you want to see what happens to children who suck their thumbs?"

She reached for a book and opened it to a picture of worms.

"If you suck on your thumb too much, tiny worms will grow in your stomach. Like this one, and this one."

Carol said "That's not true."

Nana turned the page to a picture of a tapeworm alongside of a human body. "It says right here that the worms can grow up to eighty feet long!"

Carol's eyes opened wide and she slowly removed her thumb from her mouth.

"Are there any worms inside of me right now?" She asked.

Nana replied. "There could be." Carol looked down at her stomach.

"But do you know what can get rid of them?"

"No, what?"

"Ginger cookies!"

"Really?" Carol asked in wonderment.

"Yes, worms hate Ginger cookies."

"You have Ginger cookies, Nana."

"Yes I do."

Off they went to the kitchen. Nana popped the top off the tin box of Ginger cookies and gave Carol two.

"Now it is time for you to go to bed. Let's head upstairs."

Carol put on her pajamas and hugged Nana. "I love you Nana."

"Good night little one," Nana said stroking Carol's back until she fell asleep.

Carol gently raised her thumb to her mouth as she drove.

When Carol arrived home, she found there was more turmoil than should be at the death of an 86-year-old woman. Apparently Tess, Ruth and Grace had determined that Betty had not called them in time to be with Nana when she died. They believed she died alone, whereas actually she was awake when Betty arose that morning and checked on her, and then she drifted back to sleep and on to her death.

Betty had called each sister right away, once she realized that Nana had died. She had called Doc Ely who came and confirmed the death. Betty asked each sister if they wanted to come to see Nana before Mr. Jewett took the body. No one expressed the need to do so, so Betty called Mr. Jewett. Then she had called Carol.

As far as Betty knew, there was not a problem and she met with Mr. Jewett to plan the funeral service. After her meeting, she called Mae. Frank answered the telephone. "Oh, hi Betty," he said, "I'll get Mae."

Betty could hear talking in the background and finally Mae came to the phone. She sounded flustered. "I can't talk to you, Betty. Grace will be mad at me if I do."

"Why, Mae? Have I done something wrong?"

"I just can't talk to you. If Grace finds out…"

"Mae, what is it?"

"I have to hang up." And she did.

Betty immediately called Hazel. "What is going on? Mae says she can't talk to me as Grace will be mad at her."

Hazel, smart enough to play both sides, said, "Grace has issued her orders not to have anything to do with you because you let Nana die alone. She says we should all have been called to come when she was dying. She says you ignored Nana and did not treat her well."

Betty gulped. "So you will talk to me? You do know all of that is not true? Nana died in her sleep. She was awake when I checked on her this morning, she went back to sleep, and she died then. How could I know that was going to happen?"

"Of course I will talk to you; just don't tell Grace that I have done so."

"Hazel, I loved Nana. She was like my mother! Now I have lost two mothers. Why is Grace so spiteful?"

"When have you known her not to need to be in control of everything that happens?"

Betty was now crying. "I can't believe that this is happening."

Hazel responded, "Well believe it. Grace has told us that we will not sit at the front of the church, that we are not to acknowledge you at the funeral, and afterwards we are to go to Grace's house and not back to Nana's."

Betty said tearfully, "I better go. I have things to do. Thanks for telling me." She hung up the phone.

She turned to Carol. Carol had seen her mother cry

when a pet had died but on no other occasion. "Can you believe this?" And she told Carol what was going on.

The rage started to build in Carol. The aunts had hurt her mother. "I hate them for this, Mom. They should be in mourning for Nana and not carrying on like this. I'm going to call them."

"No, leave them alone. They can't do any more damage to this family right now."

The next day the minister came to talk with and comfort my mother about Nana. Not being overly religious, my mother blurted out, "To top it off, the cat died last week." Carol laughed inside, not that the cat died because she, too, loved the cat, but because it was so characteristic of her mother! Anyway, Betty filled the minister in on Nana and some of her life. She mentioned her sisters and never insinuated there was a problem.

The funeral was scheduled for 2 PM the next day. That morning, Betty was on the telephone with Hazel when she looked out the window to the cemetery. "Oh my God!" she said "Can anything else go wrong?"

Hazel asked what had happened. Betty exclaimed, "They have set the graveside service on the wrong plot!"

She got off the phone with Hazel and called the funeral home to tell them their error. Unfortunately there was not time to move the tent and chairs, but at least the grave was dug on the right plot.

Arriving at the funeral, Betty, Ken, and Carol went into the church. Carol sighed deeply when she saw the closed casket and was grateful it was not open. She didn't think she could handle that, nor did her mother, who requested the closed casket. The sisters were clumped together in the church vestibule and turned their backs to Betty. That didn't stop her. She walked over to them. "It is good to see you all, finally," she said pleasantly. Ruth and Hazel nodded at her. The others just stared. "If you change your minds," she said, "you are welcome to come back to Nana's home after the service." And she turned and walked back to Ken and Carol. "Let's go upstairs for the service," she said.

Carol's stomach was churning. The behavior of the aunts was nauseating. It wasn't fair that it was detracting from a tribute for Nana. There were quite a few people at the service and Betty, Ken and Carol walked in and sat in the front pew. The sisters sat defiantly in the back pews. The minister talked about Nana and it was evident that he did not know her well, as he was relatively new to the Church and Nana had not attended in the time that he had been there.

Luckily he did not mention that the cat had died, Carol thought, with a slight smile.

The minister announced that there would be a gathering at Nana's house immediately following the interment. Betty wondered if Grace had invited people other than the sisters to her house. "It doesn't matter," she thought, "I will do what Nana would have wanted."

A smaller group gathered around the grave at the cemetery, including the sisters. The minster offered a prayer and the casket was lowered. Carol again felt that uncomfortable feeling in her stomach. They then headed back out of the cemetery and up the road to the house.

Guests arrived and Carol greeted each one as Betty brought out refreshments. Nana's Canasta friends came to the house, as did the Adams' from next door. Doad, Carol and Donna arrived together. It was a small group, but they shared memories of Nana. Carol thought back to the time she did something she wasn't supposed to and Nana chased her with a spatula! She had run upstairs and gone under her parents' bed. Nana used the good old line "Just wait 'til your parents get home!" It was odd that she would think about that because Nana was so good to her all the time.

Later that evening, Hazel called. "How did things go?" she asked.

"Fine." Betty responded.

"Did many come?" Hazel asked.

"Yes, anyone who really cared about Nana was here."

Hazel heard her make her point. "I couldn't come, Betty. Grace's wrath is something no one wants to experience. She can be downright mean."

"Really?" Betty said sarcastically. "She's your sister and you have to decide where your loyalty is. Nana never would have wanted to have this happen. You all make this ten times worse than it already is."

"I know you are hurt, and I understand that. I guess time may heal this."

"Maybe." Betty hung up the phone.

Nana had left the house and farmlands to Betty and $5000 to Carol. Grace had complained about that. "I am going to contest Helen's will," Grace told Tess and Ruth.

"Why would you do that?" they were shocked.

"Because of the way Betty treated Helen. After all Helen did for her since her mother died, you would think she would be a grateful child rather than going after everything Helen had."

"All Helen had was the land and a bit saved that she left to Carol."

"Carol is a brat. If only Helen knew that! I could use that money. And I want the house and property. There is over 100 acres of prime Connecticut land. Once a developer gets ahold of that…"

"Wait!" Ruth spoke firmly. "Betty loves that land. It will never be developed. She has said that many times. Betty loves Lyme and she does not want to see it further developed."

"That may be your opinion but I am going to the Town Hall today and file to contest the will. I am a closer relation to Helen than is Betty, and the courts will give it to me. At the very least it should be left to all of us in equal shares." Grace didn't add that she felt she should get the Lion's share because she was doing all the work.

Tess just shook her head. "You should leave well enough alone. Helen's wishes should be honored."

Hazel had come in during the conversation and had been holding her tongue. Now she spoke. "You say Betty and Carol were terrible to Helen. Quite the contrary, my dear. You know you are just making all of that up."

Grace retorted, "You know everything, don't you

Hazel? Don't you think I know you have been sneaking around seeing Betty? You are playing one against the other. That is a dangerous game. I advise you to stay away from Betty."

Grace left in a huff and pointed her car in the direction of the Town Hall. "I WILL win this round, or die trying!" She exclaimed.

That Spring Betty put the farmhouse and pastures up for sale. The 100 acres remained untouched other than a house lot for Betty and Ken.

Carol enrolled at Penn State to pursue her master's degree in journalism for Fall of 1971. During the few months between the funeral and the sale of the house and land, Betty had encountered one or more of the sisters in a store and had spoken to them each time. They turned away and ignored her. Hazel continued to talk to her on the phone and Betty was allowed to visit at Hazel's as long as it wasn't a time that Grace might see her car or come over.

When the house sold, this angered Grace, and therefore the sisters. "All she wanted was to get that place sold so she could build her own house. She didn't care about Nana," Grace said to whomever would listen. "She couldn't even wait a year!"

Grace added, "If I were one of the Adams' I would really object. That property was all their Uncle Hal's and it went to a different family. And add to it that 100 aces in the woods behind the Irvine house and up to Meeting House Hill…well, Betty certainly inherited well."

Betty and Ken went forward with Alberta Pfeiffer, a local architect, to design the home that Roger Hazer would build. As the farmhouse and fields had sold, they moved to a rental at the beach in Old Lyme for a year while the house was being built on the land in the woods (coincidentally next to Ruth's house) on Sterling City Road. Carol graduated from Russell Sage College in May 1971 and moved to the rental with them for the summer. While she was home her mother insisted that she continue to go to visit with the aunts. Because it meant so much to Betty, Carol agreed to do so, but she would not visit Grace. She found Hazel, Mae, Tess and Ruth to be welcoming to her and she felt that she was doing the right thing.

Betty and Ken had to be out of the house by August 31, and it was a huge job. The majority of the furniture needed to go into storage as the beach house was furnished. They did all the moving primarily by themselves. Carol worked at a children's camp in the Adirondacks on Silver Lake in the summer and after the season she came home to help. On her first trip out of the house carrying a pile of clothes, she turned her ankle and down she went. Ken took the clothes and put them in the car. Then Carol drove the car to the beach house and limped in to sit with ice on her ankle. Soon her father arrived to take her to the clinic for x-rays. Nothing was broken but the pain was incredible. She felt useless to her parents in their efforts for the final move.

They settled into the beach house, and after two weeks Carol set off for Penn State. Betty went back to teaching and Ken continued to work at UARCO in Deep River. Hazel maintained contact with Betty but the others retained their aloofness. Betty knew that Mae was in a quandary: she was so sweet and innocent, but definitely afraid of Grace. So Betty didn't want to make things difficult for Mae and stayed away. She sent birthday cards and Christmas cards to them, but they did not reciprocate. She learned of their activities and health through Carol's visits when she came home, and through Hazel, the fence-sitter.

CHAPTER TWENTY-ONE

Jonesie

The first dead body that Carol ever saw belonged to Frank Jones, Mae's husband. It was very unusual that that would be the case when she was 23 years old. Betty did not feel that she would be welcome at the funeral so she sent flowers and sent Carol as well. When Carol entered the funeral home, she saw Mae sitting in the front row with Grace and Ruth. She sat down behind them. Then she looked forward and there he was. "Dead," she thought. "So that is what dead looks like."

Carol reached out to put a hand on Mae's shoulder. "I am so sorry, Mae," she whispered in her ear. Carol did not feel especially close to Frank, but he was a good man to Mae. All of a sudden she knew what she had to do. She leaned forward and said to Grace, "Please be sure Mae knows that my mother sent flowers." Mae's eyesight was poor and she would have to rely on someone to read the cards that came with the flowers.

This was the first time Carol had spoken to Grace since Nana died. Grace turned and looked at Carol over her shoulder. In a truly venomous tone, Grace said "Whatever would make you think that I would not tell her that?" Carol sat back in her chair and tried to hold back the tears that were coming. She thought of her mother, not welcome at a family funeral, and the tears were those of anger. As the service continued for poor dead Frank, Carol held back sobs that threatened to erupt for the hurt that Grace had caused her mother.

The service was relatively short and the minister was the only one to speak. He talked of "Jonesie's" love for the town of Ivoryton and his service through his store. He spoke of Mae's devotion to him and of him to her and told how they had met so many years ago at the Hamburg Fair.

When the service ended, Carol raced outside and burst into tears. Mary Jane and Bob Lee were there and tried to console her as she tried to tell them what a bitch Grace had been to her mother and all of the things Grace had done to cause hurt. "Do you see that my mother is not here?" she cried. "Why do you think that is?"

Although they tried to console Carol, Grace had too much power for them to believe the truths that Carol was trying to expose. Her frustrations with the family were awful. She knew Ruth and Tess were watching her, shaking their heads.

Grace had won another round, and non-family members thought Carol was chief mourner for Frank Jones.

During this scene, Mae still sat in front of the casket, and Grace stuck close. "Grace," Mae asked. "Was Carol here?"

"Yes," Grace said.

"Betty's girl?" Mae asked.

"Yes, Mae." Grace said.

"That's good," said Mae.

Within a few weeks of Frank's death, Grace decided

that it would be best for Mae to move "across the river" and live with Tess and D.G.. Certainly they would not want to spend money on a nursing home, and with Mae's limited eyesight, she needed some help. Grace informed Tess that she would take Mae in and Mae would pay her monthly. Despite Mae's wishes, which she would not express to Grace, Mae was given a bed in the living room that was rarely used, in the Early Dawn farmhouse.

Mae was far from an invalid, but her vision restricted how much she could help Tess and D.G. in the home. She had known Tess was frugal with the tea, but she also found out that Tess would not turn on the heat unless there was a danger of pipes freezing. Mae begged for heat and told Tess she would pay the bills but Tess refused. "Put on sweaters, Mae. It doesn't make sense to pay for heat when we can just dress warmer."

Despite lacking the luxury of heat, and there would be a fire burning in the kitchen fireplace in the winter, Mae was always cheerful when Carol visited. She was interested in hearing what Carol knew of the news around town. Tess would serve watered down tea. At this point, Carol was living and teaching physical education in Lake Placid, New York, and would come home to visit every few week-ends.

Carol had been renting in Lake Placid, but was very

excited to tell everyone that she had just contracted to buy her own house. It was a small, two bedroom chalet that she would share with her cat and her dog. It was in a development outside of the village called Deerwood Hills, and if she stood on her roof she could see the ski jumps that were originally built for the 1932 Olympics. She would have a wooded lot of two and a half acres. She loved her job and had made many friends.

Betty and Ken had been in their new home since 1972 when Carol had moved to Lake Placid. They were enjoying the house and land. Hazel was the only sister who had seen it, and only because Betty picked her up and drove her there to visit. Hazel could not take the chance of driving there and having Ruth see her car in the driveway. It was now 1976 and this feud had been on-going since 1971.

When Carol returned to Lake Placid after her visit with Mae and Tess, she received a letter with Ruth's return address. There was a check for $100 made out to Carol and a note from Ruth saying that Mae wanted her to buy something for her new house. Carol was totally surprised and called Tess' house right away. When Tess put Mae on the telephone, Carol thanked her and Mae said "I have always been very fond of you."

Carol replied, "Well, I love you." This was a response

that not many conservative Connecticut Yankees used unless it was intimate! It probably surprised Mae quite a bit.

In June of 1976, when he was 87, D.G. died after a long illness, in the Saybrook Convalescent Home. Tess had not been able to care for him at home, and she had Mae as well. At the time of his death, D.G. had eight grandchildren and eleven great grandchildren. He had lived to see his grandson, Gary, become an integral part of Reynolds Garage and Marine.

The funeral was a large one as the Reynolds family was well known in the area. It was a graveside service in the Lyme church cemetery where Don was interred next to his first wife, Kate. Tess was the consummate widow, relieved that his suffering was over, but also sad to lose her companion of twenty years. Grace, as usual, was at her side, supporting her in her loss.

The family and friends gathered at Doad's house after the funeral where D.G.'s daughters and granddaughters had prepared a potluck meal. Leland brandished a bottle of whiskey in his father's honor. The men of the family partook of the whiskey, while the women had wine or tea. It was a noisy affair with all of the family united in honor of D.G.

Tess and Mae lived at the Early Dawn Farm for the next year. They were 83 and 88 years old, respectively.

They went through the year and the winter with the help of D.G.'s son and grandsons bringing in wood for the fireplace. Tess was doing the cooking and housekeeping. In June, 1977, Tess died at Lawrence and Memorial Hospitals after a short illness. It was decided, again by Grace, that Mae would have to go into a home and she therefore took up residence in Ferrypoint Convalescent Hospital in Old Saybrook.

In September of 1977, Mae died. Then there were only three sisters left.

CHAPTER TWENTY-TWO

So once there were eleven and now there were three. In 1977, Ruth was 80 years old, Hazel was 78, and Grace was 75. One would think that this would be a good time to settle the family feud and let Betty help them in their old age times. Clarence and Al were still living as well, and these five represented the nucleus left surrounding that generation of Hardings.

Betty still spoke when she saw them, and Ruth and Grace always turned away. Carol still visited with Ruth and Hazel when she was in town. Although there were a lot of second cousins in the family, Carol was the one who had been raised with all of the aunts, and had been taught to respect them and share time with all of them. Carol's cousins knew all of the aunts but not equally well as families have different allegiances and they spent more time with different aunts.

As Ruth aged, she was "adopted" by Laura and Leland Reynolds, who helped her with doctor appointments and other needs. Carol Reynolds Dunham became her financial guardian. In the Winter of 1980, it was decided by the Reynolds', and surprisingly not by Grace, that it was time for Ruth to go into Chesterfield Nursing Home. Carol was home for a visit in February and went to see Ruth at the home.

She was in a semi-private room in her bed. She recognized Carol, and said "How nice of you to come!"

Carol asked how she was feeling. "Fair to middling. It is scary here though."

"Why is that?" Carol asked.

"They keep hanging the bodies from the ceiling in the halls. Did you see them?"

"Now Ruth, we wouldn't let you be anywhere that did something like that."

Ruth looked at her wide-eyed. Carol realized that one can't argue with a delusional person and so she changed the subject.

Carol talked about how she had just returned from a trip to Jamaica. Lake Placid had just hosted the 1980 Winter Olympics and the schools had been closed. Carol had rented her house and car out to a family from New York City and used the money to go on a trip to Jamaica with friends. Ruth listened quietly.

"I have been thinking," Ruth said. "You could go to my house. In the garage there are some galvanized buckets and you could put them in a line from the driveway to the back door. Then you could come and get me and I could step from bucket to bucket and get into the house. Can you do that for me?"

Realizing that there was no way to make her see that she was talking in a nonsensical way, Carol said "Of course, I can help you."

Carol then tried to start another story and Ruth stopped her. "This is a nice visit but if you are going to get the buckets you need to get going before Mr. Janski takes the buckets away." Mr. Janski was the town garbage collector; apparently Ruth remembered him.

"Okay, Ruth, I will go take care of that." She left, thinking it wasn't going to be long for Ruth.

Ruth died in July of 1980. Carol did not see her again after the visit in February. She had declined so much that she did not know anyone, and it was difficult to be with her. Carol did attend her funeral. Ruth was buried in the Harding family plot next to her beloved brother Lyman.

When Carol reflected on Ruth's life, she saw her as so successful at a time when women were rarely so strong and independent. What she could not understand was Ruth's subservience to Grace, and her part in the family feud. Ruth had been a principal! She was a person in charge of all the teachers and the children under her supervision. She had been a board member and treasurer of the church, a trusted position. She was well-respected in the community. Being single, she had no one to care for her, and it would have been very logical that Betty would have been an asset to her. But she listened to Grace and she let Grace control her. Carol decided that was one question she would never have answered.

Hazel was then 81 and Grace 78. They did not get along with each other exceptionally well. Hazel was then spending a lot of time with Betty because Clarence had died and she knew Betty would take care of her. Hazel had Francis Rand cooking and bringing in dinners for her, and Betty was doing her book-work. She had a cleaning lady taking care of the house. She had a handyman of sorts to mow the lawn in summer and shovel the snow in winter. Her son, Bob, was still in Pennsylvania and came to visit occasionally, or when Betty called him and said she needed his help. That was usually when Hazel was driving Betty crazy with telephone calls!

Hazel did not really do anything with her life. She stayed home and sat on the sunporch. She did not listen to the radio or the TV, and she really didn't read much. Her lazy susan on the kitchen table was filled with pill bottles, and she loved to count her pills. It was a very lonely life for her and her only outlet was the telephone. She would live another ten years like this, remaining in her own home.

Carol went to visit whenever she was in town. She had moved to Ohio in 1982 to attend graduate school and she graduated with her Ph.D. in Motor Development, Physical Education in 1985. She then accepted a position in Physical Education Teacher Education at the University of Toledo, Toledo, Ohio. She would teach there until her retirement in 2007.

A typical visit with Hazel was always frustrating to Carol, because it seemed to her that Hazel could do more; Carol could not understand how she could sit there day after day doing nothing.

"Hi Hazel, how's it going?"

"Oh! Your mother said you were coming home to visit."

"Yes, the University is out for Spring break. I have 10 days off."

"That's nice."

"How are you?"

"Well my eyes are a problem. The eye doctor says I have dry eyes so I have to take drops."

"Can you watch TV?"

"I probably could. But I don't care much about it."

"Have you read anything good lately?"

"I don't read very much. My eyes, you know."

"Would you like a subscription to large print *Reader's Digest*?"

"That would be good."

"Okay, I will get you one. What have you heard from Bob?"

"I call him every day. He doesn't like to talk much."

Finally Carol realized what would get Hazel talking. "Hazel, tell me about growing up with all those sisters, and, of course, Lyman."

"I was the second youngest, you know. Grace was the baby and she always got her way. I guess you could say she still does. Anyway, my sisters always made me do their chores."

"Why did you do the chores for them?"

"Because I didn't want them to be mad at me. Sometimes I would go and hide behind the wall in the pasture and I would hear them calling me. I knew what they wanted and I pretended I didn't hear them. Eventually they would find me and set up some reason that I was needed to do extra chores. Then they would go off skating at the Mill Pond, or walking along Sterling City Road to visit their friends. It was mostly Tess and Ruth, but sometimes Elsie would make me do her chores too. Lyman never did. He was also treated as special because he was the only boy. I never felt that I was a favorite of Mother, but I always tried to please her. I guess there is not enough attention to go around when there are ten girls and one boy."

"I imagine not."

"That's why I had only Bob. I knew we could give him all the attention he needed and he would be happy. We didn't even ask him to do chores! He liked to follow Clare into the workshop and help there when he could. Then when Helen came here to live, we had two teenagers! But there was enough attention for both of them."

"So were you and Grace close to each other, since you were the last two?"

"No! Everyone babied Grace and catered to her every whim. Grace would just make faces at me and say cruel things. We never got along very well. We are still not close but we can tolerate each other. She really was a monster. When she was in nursing school she had a baby. No one knew who the father was, and she killed the baby right after it was born."

"She killed the baby? How do you know?"

"Mae was going to adopt the baby and therefore help her out of her 'predicament.' Grace stayed away from home for a long time, and Mae had told us that she was pregnant but lost the baby – that the little girl was stillborn. I knew something was up between Grace and Mae and finally Mae told us, sitting right here at this kitchen table."

"So the baby was stillborn? Then she didn't kill the baby."

"Yes she did. A baby doesn't go to full term and then arrive stillborn. She was ashamed and panicked and killed the baby. I know she did. Grace is mean. She can't hide the truth from me, though."

In November of 1989, Grace died in a nursing home in Waterford, CT. There was a funeral but Carol and Betty did not attend. Al would now be free to live the life that everyone suspected he would like to live. He had many male friends that he went to visit, both when he was working and after he retired. He had spent 55 years of listening to Grace telling him what to do when, and now he was free.

The next September, Hazel died at home. Carol was not able to come home for the funeral. She was amused to hear, however, that the telephone rang at the funeral service. That was Hazel's last call.

EPILOGUE

The houses still stand on Sterling City Road, although Hazel's and Ruth's have been renovated and have had several owners. The old Harding Homestead has also been re-done and has seen many owners, it is a beautiful place. The Martin house remains almost the same and is on its fourth owner. There had been some interior work done and an addition has been built between Nana's kitchen and the old woodshed to extend the kitchen area.

The family feud was never resolved and it was the aunts' loss that they did not embrace Betty. She would have helped them in any way they needed. She knew the importance of family.

When Carol visits, she often walks through the cemetery. She sees the Martin stone where Hal and Nana are buried. Betty's name is on the stone as well, "Elizebeth B. Plimpton, 1921-1994." Betty was cremated and as per her wishes, her ashes were scattered over the ledge on the property behind her house. Carol goes to the Harding stone, and sees the graves of her great grandparents, her great uncles Lyman Noah and Lyman Darius, and her great aunt Ruth. She goes by the Reynolds stone and on to the Peck grave, where Bill and Tess are resting. And finally she goes to the Lee stone, for Hazel and Clarence. She never visits the Hendry stone; even though Grace and Al lie adjacent to the Lee graves, Carol turns her back.

Carol always hikes with her dog up to the ledge, and she sits, looking out at Hamburg Cove and the Connecticut River, and she talks with her mother. She imagines that Betty hears every word and she is sure that there is a special presence surrounding her.